LEATHER
JEWELRY

LEATHER JEWELRY

30 CONTEMPORARY PROJECTS

Nathalie Mornu

LARK BOOKS

A Division of Sterling Publishing Co., Inc.
New York / London

Art Director
Kristi Pfeffer

Photography Director
Dana Irwin

Photography
Lynne Harty, principal
Steve Mann, pages 8–32
Stewart O'Shields, pages 9–12

Illustrations
Olivier Rollin

Editorial Assistant
Kathleen McCafferty

Cover Design
Chris Bryant

Library of Congress Cataloging-in-Publication Data

Mornu, Nathalie.
  Leather jewelry : 30 contemporary projects / Nathalie Mornu. -- 1st ed.
     p. cm.
  Includes index.
  ISBN 978-1-60059-529-5 (pb-trade pbk. : alk. paper)
  1. Leatherwork. 2. Jewelry making. I. Title.
  TT290.M62 2010
  739.27--dc22

                         2009030532

10 9 8 7 6 5 4 3 2 1

First Edition

Published by Lark Books, A Division of
Sterling Publishing Co., Inc.
387 Park Avenue South, New York, NY 10016

Text © 2010, Lark Books, a Division of Sterling Publishing Co., Inc.

Photography © 2010, Lark Books, A Division of Sterling Publishing Co., Inc.,
unless otherwise specified

Illustrations © 2010, Lark Books, A Division of Sterling Publishing Co., Inc.,
unless otherwise specified

Distributed in Canada by Sterling Publishing,
c/o Canadian Manda Group, 165 Dufferin Street
Toronto, Ontario, Canada M6K 3H6

Distributed in the United Kingdom by GMC Distribution Services,
Castle Place, 166 High Street, Lewes, East Sussex, England BN7 1XU
Distributed in Australia by Capricorn Link (Australia) Pty Ltd.,
P.O. Box 704, Windsor, NSW 2756 Australia

If you have questions or comments about this book, please contact:

Lark Books
67 Broadway, Asheville, NC 28801
828-253-0467

Manufactured in China

ISBN 13: 978-1-60059-529-5

For information about custom editions, special sales, or premium and corporate purchases, please contact the Sterling Special Sales Department at 800-805-5489 or specialsales@sterlingpub.com.

For information about desk and examination copies available to college and university professors, requests must be submitted to academic@larkbooks.com. Our complete policy can be found at www.larkbooks.com.

THE PROJECTS

When you think of leather jewelry, do images of hippies wearing wristlets tooled with floral designs spring to mind? Or bad-ass bikers wearing black armbands strapped on with buckles? Punkers bristling with spiked cuffs? Or crafts you made at camp? That's old school. Contemporary leather jewelry looks nothing like that. Instead, it ranges from stylish to playful, from stark to frilly; it's colorful and multifaceted, it can even be sculptural. In a word, it's *modern*.

Flip through these pages and you'll see the scope of today's leather jewelry. Lassoo, on page 42, is an elegant braided loop to wear long and slinky, or wrapped twice (or even thrice) around the neck. The hot-pink Scrunch hoops on page 74 pair bold scale and interesting texture. Searching for a cool, urban accessory that's tough yet pretty? Check out the fur-covered City cuff on page 106. For a more feminine look, turn to Gleam, on page 108. In sparkling metal tones, this rose-shaped barrette can also be clipped to a hat or fastened at the neckline as a brooch. And if you want to get noticed, wear a Rollo ring (page 86)…or a handful!

If you've never made anything from leather, you may think it's like trying to manipulate cardboard; after all, leather's used to make shoes—it must be tough, right? You might figure it's almost impossible to hack through, difficult to shape, hard to assemble. Nope, *nyet*, nuh-uhn. Once you get started, you'll discover it's a versatile material that cuts like butter and is so easy to work with.

In fact, you already perfected the skills you need for fashioning leather into jewelry in preschool. If you can use scissors, pound with a hammer, button a shirt, and knot your shoelaces, you can make any of the pieces in this book. Though you'll need a bit more precision than you had at the age of five, the techniques for making the projects in this book essentially involve little beyond some cutting, a few strikes of a mallet, assembling simple mechanisms, and threading elements together.

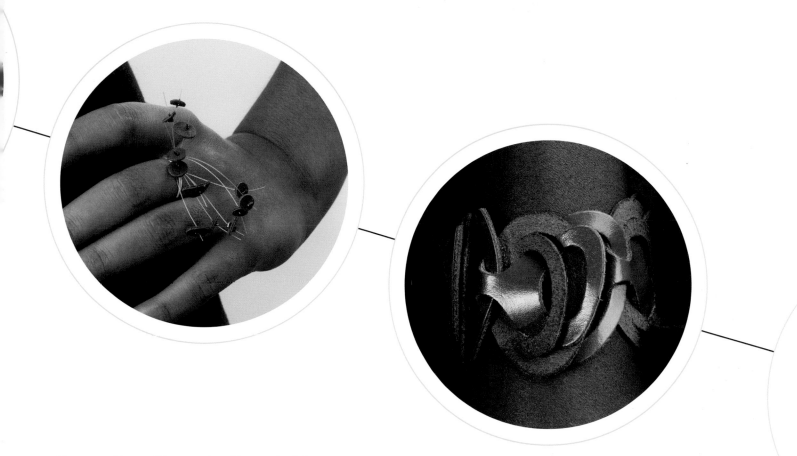

Since working with an unfamiliar material can feel slightly daunting, the first part of the book covers all the information you'll need about techniques, tools, and materials, including exotic skins. It also describes a few jewelry-making techniques, in case you've never handled jeweler's pliers. Thirty fun projects with step-by-step instructions follow, organized by category: necklaces, earrings, rings, bracelets and cuffs, and hair accessories. There's also a gallery of work by professional jewelers, so you can see exciting pieces from around the globe.

Not only is leather simple to work with, it's also pleasing to the senses: it feels good to the touch, it smells great, and it comes in an array of gorgeous colors and fantastic finishes. So pick a project to make, gather up a few tools and some luscious leather, and get ready to adorn yourself with some fabulous trinkets.

THE SKINNY ON SKINS

MATERIALS

Almost any kind of leather has the potential to become a fantastic piece of jewelry, but a given piece may not be appropriate for making a specific item. For example, you can't expect to turn a stiff piece of leather that's 6 millimeters (¼ inch) thick into Regina (page 36); this design demands a thin, supple material such as lambskin or sueded pigskin. Consider the characteristics you want in your finished bangle, necklace, or earrings, and then choose the leather accordingly. If possible, before you buy leather, handle it to see how it behaves and to gauge whether it will act the way you need it to.

Very few of the projects in this book started out as vegetable-tanned leather. Think cowboy belts and holsters—they're made from vegetable-tanned leather. This material comes in a plain flesh color and can be rigid, especially in heavier weights. Although its surface is a blank canvas very receptive to transformations such as tooling, carving, branding, molding, and dyeing, I decided not to focus on it for this book.

Instead, most of the jewelry in this book is made from garment- or upholstery-grade leather. This type of leather is processed with chemical compounds and could never be mistaken for vegetable-tanned leather. The project designers chose it either for its color or for the way it drapes. It's more flexible and comes in a wide range of surface types, from smooth to embossed; in hues from natural tones to electric shades found infrequently in nature; and in all kinds of finishes, such as metallic and crackle. It acts much like fabric and, depending on its thickness, stitches up pretty easily.

Vegetable-tanned leather

Because leather is such a thin material, and its thickness can vary by subtle amounts, it's more accurate to describe the thickness in millimeters than in inches. In case you're more familiar with the standard system, in this section, metric measurements are roughly converted.

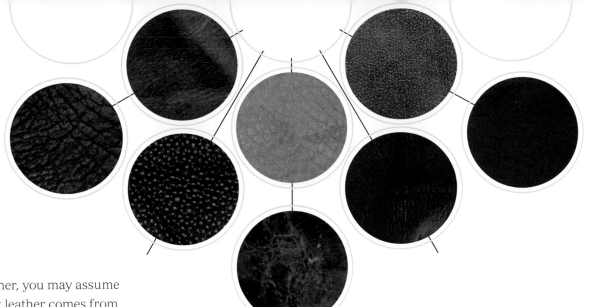

Common Leathers

When you think of leather, you may assume cowhide or pigskin, but leather comes from many different sources. Leathers derived from smaller animals are called skins; the ones that come from larger animals are hides. The thinnest, softest, most pliable leathers come from smaller animals and include goatskin, lambskin, calfskin, and deerskin. Women's gloves, for example, tend to be made from these skins.

One of the great qualities of cowhide, which has a smooth grain side and a sueded side, is that it's usually dyed all the way through. You can use either side, so you get two textures from a single purchase.

Leather Lingo

Full grain is the natural surface of the leather; it isn't altered in any way, meaning that scars, scratches, and wrinkles show. To hide these imperfections, leather can be buffed, much as wood is sanded. When project instructions in this book refer to the grain, that means the smooth side of the leather—the right side, the one meant to show, the side with a special finish.

Suede is technically the flesh side of leather opposite the grain; it has a velvety appearance. But because there's also a leather commonly called suede (shown at right), to avoid confusion, this book refers to the back side of leather as the wrong side.

The thickness of hides varies; to get them a consistent thickness, they're fed grain-side up through a splitting machine. The topmost layer, which retains

the grain, is called top grain. The underlayer (or under-layers, if there's enough for more than one) is known as a split or a sueded split, because it has a sueded texture on both sides. When a project in this book calls for suede, it means a sueded split. Because it doesn't contain any fibers to hold it together, suede has less structural strength. In cows, unsplit hides average a thickness of 4.8 millimeters ($3/16$ inch). Upholstery leathers range from 0.9 to 1.6 millimeters ($1/32$ to $1/16$ inch) in thickness.

With stamping or embossing, a pattern is applied under heat and pressure to make a cowhide or other leather resemble something different, usually a more exotic skin.

Manufacturers create all kinds of fancy leathers for footwear, handbags, and various upscale products. With its high-gloss appearance, for example, patent leather is yummy stuff. Other surface treatments include:

* Distressing or crackle finishes
* Pearlized finishes
* Metallic finishes
* Foils applied to imitate exotic skins such as lizard

* Glazes that give a soft, hazy shine
* Milling to give special textures
* Stamped or embossed designs, such as Western motifs or faked ostrich or crocodile, applied under heat and pressure
* Complex punched patterns
* Printing and tie-dyeing
* The permanent application of fabrics to the upper surface of the leather
* Varnishes
* Laser cutting, both to "engrave" linear designs and to create lacy cutwork

These top finishes are applied to the grain sides of all types of leathers, from cowhide to lambskin. It's rare to come across scraps of especially fancy leathers that make you swoon, but you may see manufactured items you're willing to buy and cut up just for their amazing leather.

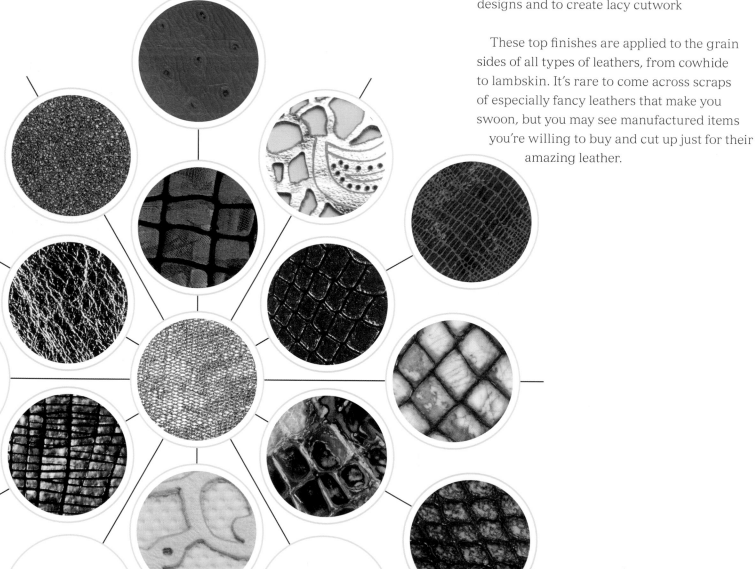

Exotic Skins

All leathers have distinct grains or characteristics. Using exotic skins in your jewelry will probably require a higher financial investment, and a greater challenge to locate them, but it will *so* pay off in the visual punch of the jewelry. However, you may find it easier to locate lambskin or cowhide that's been faked to look like exotics.

Crocodile or alligator **A** has an armored appearance, with large, rectangular scales that are sometimes raised. Depending on where it was taken from the animal, this leather can be too tough for the designs in this book, but that doesn't mean you can't come up with designs of your own.

Eelskin **B** is soft and deeply lustrous, with a unique textured stripe running down its center. Because it comes from a long, slender fish, the skin comes in narrow strips. Eel is frequently used to make wallets and purses, and it's recognizable due to the striped effect of the patched panels.

Fishskin **C** includes the skins taken from grouper, salmon, tilapia, and other types of fish farmed for food. The fan-shaped scales have a texture that's unmistakable.

Frogskin **D** has a wonderful burnished texture with freckling. The skins are quite small, but that's not an issue when making small-scale jewelry items.

Kangaroo **E** looks much like cowhide but has a higher tensile strength, so it's good for making lacing and motorcycle leathers.

The textures of lizardskin **F** include tight geometric grids and areas of rectangular scales.

Depending on where it came off the bird, ostrich has two different appearances. Skin from the leg resembles that of lizard, while ostrich hide has interesting nubs, almost like moles, spaced wide apart to create a texture you won't see anywhere else **G**. Some people consider ostrich one of the finest and most durable leathers available.

Sharkskin **H** looks something like sandpaper, coarse and wrinkled and heavy, with a matte finish, but to the touch, it just feels like stiff leather.

Snakeskin **I** has two interesting features—its scaliness, and the play of light and dark camouflage markings on the skin. On python, this is called the diamond effect. Its natural earth tones can be bleached and dyed.

Stingray **J** looks and feels like tiny glass beads, with a pale, cigar-shaped area at the center of the skin. It's also known as shagreen. Manufacturers sometimes dye it and then sand off a minute amount of the upper layer, leaving behind a distinctive field of colored cell walls enclosing white.

Be sure to purchase exotic skins from reputable dealers; definitely don't support businesses that threaten endangered animal species by carrying their skins.

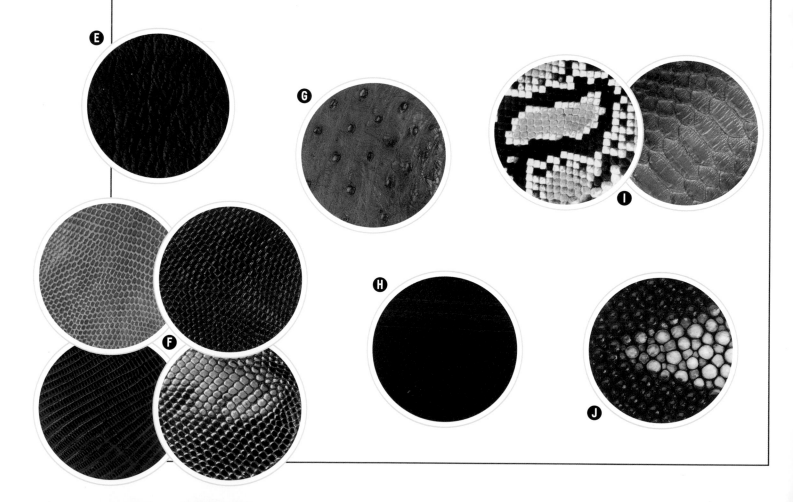

Locating Leather

As ubiquitous as leather items seem to be—there's no shortage of shoes, wallets, belts, and purses around, right?—tracking down the raw material requires a bit of resourcefulness, especially because you don't need a large quantity for jewelry making.

The obvious place to look is hobby stores; most will have a small leather department. Specialty leather outlets are few and far between unless you live in a major metropolitan area, but if you look online using a search term such as "leather hobby," you'll come across more retailers than you would in your local phone book. They'll be glad to send you catalogs, and these are the go-to places for leather-working tools, dyes, and hardware. Some saddle shops stock tools, dyes, and hardware, too, and will sell you vegetable-tanned leather.

The Internet is a terrific resource for all kinds of fancy leathers, skins, and furs. Depending on what you want, use variations of the search terms "leather," "hides," "skins," "bookbinding leather," and "exotic skins." You can also look on online auction sites, which give you the option of doing very specific searches.

Closer to home, you can generally find suede elbow patches in the notions department of fabric stores, but they come in ho-hum colors. Talk to the clerks, though. Many fabric stores stock whole hides in the upholstery section, and they may also have big bins of scraps sold by weight, or the salespeople may know of other places to find scrap leather. Speaking of uphol-stering, check with furniture stores; they may be willing to give you old sample books of leather from last year's models. Ask around at the body shops that pimp out cars and bikes, too; if they upholster seats, there's a good chance they've

BARBARA COHEN | *Ring*
Dyed fox fur, sterling silver, foam, gold, pearl
PHOTO BY ARTIST

got scraps they'll give away or sell. Shoe-repair shops may sell you small quantities of leather, but it might not be the most malleable stuff.

If you're in a metropolitan area with a garment district, check for leather wholesalers; be aware you'll have to buy entire hides from them, and they do get pricey!

Finally, hunt around thrift stores for leather items such as old skirts, jackets, or vintage kidskin gloves to repurpose and cut up. You can also take apart old or new wallets, purses, or toss pillows, if you think the price is right.

Most likely, though, you're going to make jewelry from factory scraps or smaller pieces cut from hides. Look them over before use: make sure they don't have flaws, discoloration, or marks, and check them for stretch. If you've ever sewn, you know that fabric has a grain. Leather has it too, both in the sense of full-grain leather (as in an unbuffed surface) and in the sense of elasticity. Commercial manufacturers of leather goods typically discard the areas of the hides that distend too much—using them in a product could affect its quality and longevity— so those end up in the scrap bins at fabric stores. Therefore, when you come across larger pieces in there, pull on them in all directions to check whether they stretch, and particularly whether they stretch too much.

Size Matters

Although fabric is measured in yards, leather doesn't come off a mill and can't conform to standard widths. Therefore, the size of leather is calculated by its area in square feet (or meters). You don't usually need a lot of leather for jewelry, but if you're concerned about making something large, be careful when you buy sight unseen: a square foot of leather doesn't necessarily measure 12 by 12 inches. It might be 24 inches long and only 6 inches wide, which may or may not matter for your project.

Weight Versus Thickness

Because leather is an organic material, it's not necessarily a uniform thickness so, long ago, tanners began designating the thickness of leather by weight, in ounces. One-ounce leather weighed 1 ounce per square foot; 2-ounce leather weighed 2 ounces per square foot; you get the picture. But what did that mean? How thick was 2-ounce leather? It required gobs of experience handling different types of leathers for it to make any sense. If this jargon seems indecipherable to you, you're not alone!

These days, although the thickness of leather is still quoted in ounces, the American industry has instituted a standard: each ounce indicates a thickness of 0.4 millimeter (1/64 inch)—just do the math. For crafters, it would be far more useful to just assign a measurement in millimeters, but because you'll frequently come across leather labeled and sold in ounces, you'll need to know something about what that means.

The thinnest leathers are 1 to 2 ounces. Those will be the most malleable, and they're about 0.4 to 0.8 millimeter (1/64 to 1/32 inch) thick. At 0.9 to 1 millimeter in thickness, garment leathers just squeak into this category. Upholstery leathers and those for outer garments tend to weigh in at 3 to 4 ounces; if you've ever handled chaps, they're made from about that thickness, which runs from 1.2 to 1.6 millimeters (3/64 to 1/16 inch). The most rugged leathers, like those used for harnesses and carpenters' belts, are 4 to 4.4 millimeters (5/32 to 11/64 inch); they're labeled as 10 or 11 ounces.

Flexibility

Just to confuse the issue a wee bit more, depending on how they were processed and finished, leathers of the same thickness can exhibit different rigidities. A thin leather might be as limp as an evening glove, or it could be stiff, almost like card stock. This affects how the leather handles for a given jewelry design. For example, you want the most flexible suede you can find to make Gossip (page 59); rigid lacing wouldn't knot tightly, and the ends would stick up awkwardly, making for a silly-looking necklace.

Choosing Leather for this Book

The materials lists for the projects in this book give information about the optimal type of leather to use to replicate the item shown in the photo. First, you'll see how much leather you need, which type, and the color (which, of course, is really up to you). Next, you'll learn whether the project designer used a soft leather—one that's supple—or a firm, stiff leather. Finally, there's the thickness, in millimeters, of the actual leather used for the jewelry item shown, followed by its equivalent in ounces; that way, you can tell whether the leather you're considering using for your own jewelry will fit the bill—whether it's sold in ounces or is a scrap whose thickness you need to measure.

You don't have to get too worked up about exactly matching what the designer used. Handle your leather before using it for a project; compare how it looks and drapes to the project photos to make sure you think it'll work for the piece you want to create. For all the projects calling for garment-weight leather, you can use garment-tanned cow, calf, goat, kid, lamb, pig, or deer. Again, don't get bogged down in specifics. If your leather looks like it can do what's shown in the project photo, it probably can.

TANIA CLARKE HALL | *Necklace*
Cowhide, paint
PHOTOS BY PAUL KING

Hair-On Hides and Fur

Hair-on hides include numerous animals, but you're most likely to find (and be able to afford) cow that's been printed to look like other skins, such as leopard, zebra, or giraffe. Like vegetable-tanned leather, hair-on hides tend to be stiff. So what? The fur looks so cool that it's worth designing around that characteristic. It's perfect for flat items such as cuffs.

For fur, try to recycle trims from gloves and vintage garments. Some craft stores sell rabbit skins, dyed or not, and some sell fur pompons.

Always cut hair-on hides and fur from the wrong (or back) side, aiming as much as possible to cut only the hide, not the hair or fur.

Cord, Lacing, and Strips

Because manufacturers aren't consistent with their nomenclature, you'll come across all these names for the same product. To help keep things straight, in this book anything described as cord has a round cross-section, while lacing (also called lace) is flat or square. These come in many colors and in a few different sizes, sold in packages or on rolls, where you buy them by the yard. If you can, feel cords and lacings before you buy them; try to avoid anything rigid. It's harder to work with, and it looks stiff in a project.

Cleaning

If you're worried about dirt, keep in mind that smooth leather is more resistant to soiling than leather with a rough surface. Clean smooth surfaces with saddle soap and a damp—not wet—cloth. Most dirt will come off just by wiping. For suede, use a soft brush and suede cleaner.

Storage

Store leather flat whenever possible. If you have especially large pieces and no place to keep them flat, don't fold them: instead, roll them up. If the leather you buy has creases, place a heavy book over the affected areas for a few days to get the folds out. (If that doesn't work, see Removing Creases on page 24.)

Hardware

Some of the projects in this book were designed with leather-specific hardware, but others use jewelry-making findings, obtainable from beading stores and jewelers' catalogs, as well as other useful odds and ends that you can source from different places.

Eyelets serve a functional purpose—reinforcing holes so they don't tear—sure, but they can also add a dash of visual interest. Those designed for leatherwork come strictly in metallic tones and accommodate thicker leathers. However, if you're working with lightweight leather, you can probably use the eyelet type sold in fabric stores, where you'll find a larger selection of sizes and shades. You'll discover an even wider assortment of eyelet colors in the scrapbooking section of your local crafts store, but these should be reserved for use on only the thinnest leathers.

Grommets reinforce holes, too. What's the difference between the two? A grommet consists of two components, an eyelet and a washer; a grommet has a wider flange, in relation to its hole, than an eyelet does, and therefore has more strength. Because it's a beefier piece of hardware, it looks more industrial.

Snaps come in two types. The kind sold for leatherwork is a post style; it has a shaft that requires you to punch a hole to penetrate the leather. These snaps come in a variety of metal finishes, and you can even find a few with tuff designs such as stars or eagle heads on the cap.

The prong-style snap has teeth capable of piercing fabric or lightweight leather. You can buy this sort of snap in fabric stores.

All snaps consist of four-part mechanisms. The parts are not interchangeable, so if you have

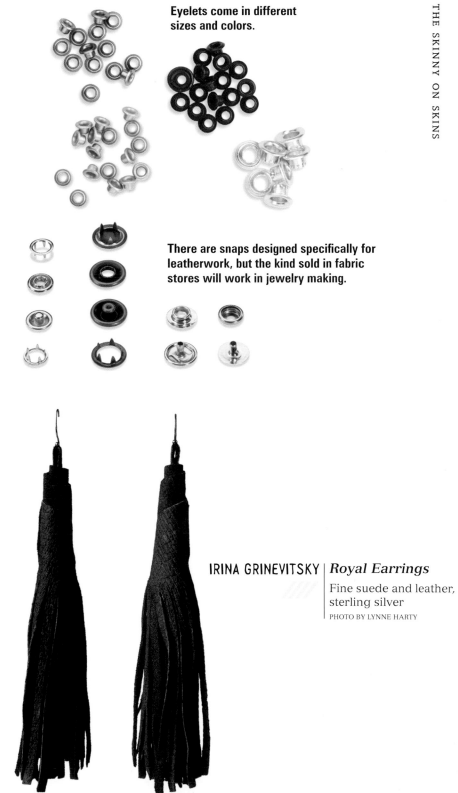

Eyelets come in different sizes and colors.

There are snaps designed specifically for leatherwork, but the kind sold in fabric stores will work in jewelry making.

IRINA GRINEVITSKY | *Royal Earrings*

Fine suede and leather, sterling silver

PHOTO BY LYNNE HARTY

Rivets connect two pieces of leather permanently, so be sure to punch your holes in the right place.

JOSEPHINE BERGSØE | *Cuff*
///// Nile crocodile, keshi pearl, diamond, gold
PHOTO BY KRISTIAN GRANQUIST

more than one kind on hand, don't mix them during installation!

Rivets aren't closures; they connect two pieces of leather permanently. A series of them can punctuate or emphasize a design. Manufacturers make them in different sizes and assorted metal finishes, including silver, brass, and antique nickel. You can get domed rivets as well as diamond- and pyramid-shaped ones. There are rivets whose caps are engraved with designs such as a flower or a star. Another type is the double-cap rivet, which, once mounted, looks finished on both sides. And you can add a bunch of bling with fancy, ornamental rivets topped with faceted crystals or polished synthetic stones. Rivets require a special rivet-setting kit.

The designers in this book gussied up their projects with all kinds of cool findings. These are the types of things you'll find in bead stores or jewelry catalogs, stuff like beading wire, beads, bead caps, and cones. You can get head pins, jump rings, split rings, bars (see Coco,

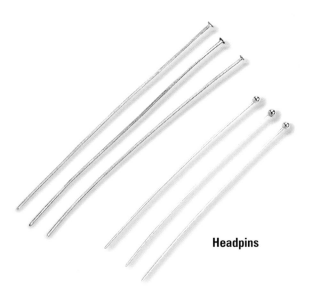

Headpins

page 39), and crimp beads in all sorts of metals; look for warm copper and brass, dramatic gunmetal, cool silver, or elegant gold. Ear wires even come in every shade of the rainbow when they're made from anodized aluminum! Chain and clasps, too, come in all metal finishes and a wide assortment of styles, from delicate to chunky. When you select your findings, bring along the leather. Hold the findings up against it to see whether you like the combination of colors and tones.

Once upon a time, you may have had to look a little harder for ring backs and pin backs, but not anymore with the Internet. Finally, you can use the barrette backs sold by craft retailers, or go with the low-profile styles stocked in the hair products department of your favorite grocery or drug store.

Adhesives

Leather outlets sell leather cement as well as all-purpose cement and contact cement, and thinners for them. Household cement does a good job, too. The project designers in this book list their own favorite adhesives in the instructions. No matter which type you choose, don't fry your brain cells while using it: always work in a well-ventilated area.

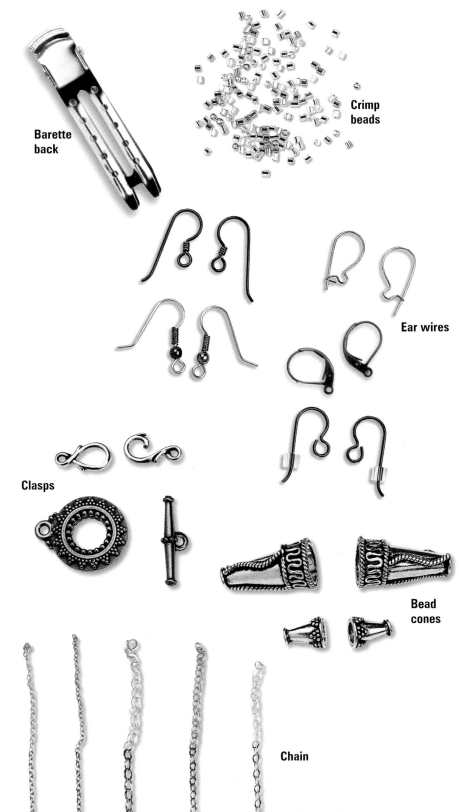

Barette back

Crimp beads

Ear wires

Clasps

Bead cones

Chain

TOOLS

You probably already have many of the tools listed here. A few are specialized for leatherwork. Familiarize yourself with them before starting your project.

Cutting

Before I started working with leather, it seemed sturdier than the cardboard used for boxes; because that material is hard to hack through, it appeared logical that leather would be even more challenging to cut. Instead, the first time I cut leather, I was astounded at how easy it was to slice. Professional leatherworkers use trimming knives, round knives, and head knives designed specifically for working with leather—their shape has changed little over the centuries, and in fact images of these tools appear on the walls of ancient Egyptian tombs—but you don't need to invest in these. Any large, sharp, sewing shears should slice through leather easily.

Cutting leather will dull the blades, though, so dedicate a pair of them to leatherwork, or be prepared to have the shears sharpened when you want to resume sewing with them.

A few of the projects were cut with pedicure scissors, but using them is optional. Their benefit derives from the ratio of short blade to long handle, which makes it easy to control the cutting of tight curves accurately. Note that we're not talking about the cheap clippers you can find at any drugstore. These high-quality specialty scissors effortlessly cut through thick leather like it's butter, but they come at a price.

You probably already have a pair of cheap craft scissors around; you'll need them to snip paper and other non-fabric items.

As the name implies, scalloping shears cut a dainty scalloped edge. The scalloping scissors sold in the paper or scrapbooking section of craft stores won't do the trick. For cutting leather, you'll need the heavy-duty

Left to right: Pedicure scissors, scalloping shears, heavy-duty nippers, craft knife, box cutter, rotary cutter

kind. For some reason, nobody manufactures these anymore; luckily, they're available at online auction sites. Only two projects have scalloped edges, and if you don't want to invest in specialty scissors, you can always go with a pinked edge or even a straight one.

When it comes to straight lines, if the leather's not terribly heavy or stretchy, you can cut it with a craft knife, or use a box cutter or a utility knife for thicker leather. Always insert new blades in the tool before starting a project.

Finally, you can also use a rotary cutter, which is basically a wheel-shaped razor blade mounted on a handle—it's really sharp, so don't treat it like a toy. Always use this tool in conjunction with a self-healing mat, or you'll destroy your work surface and dull the blade faster. Rotary cutters come in a range of sizes, and they're sold in fabric and quilt shops.

Look in a hardware store or a home-improvement center for heavy-duty nippers. Use them to cut off rivets that you've assembled incorrectly, or to snip wire and other metal items.

ANDREA JANOSIK | *Red Spike, bracelet*
Suede sheepskin, leather cord, sterling silver
PHOTO BY MAIKE PAUL

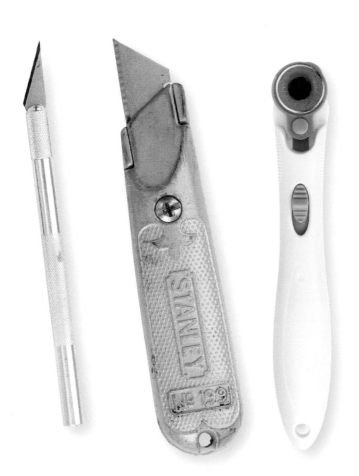

Punching

Punching accomplishes one of two things: it can cut away a hole to create negative space, or if you save the positive shape, you end up with a circle or another contour.

A rotating punch makes small round holes in a variety of sizes—usually a half dozen, depending on the model you get, which may range from a pinhole to 6 millimeters (⅞2 inch). Simply turn the wheel to select the size. You don't need a hammer; just squeeze the tool with the leather between it, as if it were pliers or a hole punch for paper. A rotating punch can only make holes near the edges of leather.

For cutting circles in a range up to 1.3 centimeters (½ inch), you can find gasket punches (also called hollow punches) at any good hardware store or online. They're cheap and easy to locate, but they dull fast. You can also get leather punches to cut small circles as well as ovals, oblongs, and conchos; you can find these through leather suppliers. They also come in larger sizes, with a price tag to match.

An awl looks exactly like an ice pick. Use it to poke holes in leather for stitching or for running other things through the material.

Pounding

Mallets have heads made from rawhide, polymer plastic, or wood, and they come in different weights. The bigger the punch and the thicker the leather, the more mass you ought to have behind the blow. Never use a metal tool, such as a hammer, to pound punches: it will ruin the cutting edge on the tool. It's fine to use a small hammer when setting eyelets and rivets.

Gasket punches

Rotating punch

High-quality leather punches don't come cheap.

Awl

Oval leather punches

I bid long and hard to win this old wooden mallet at an online auction. It's five pounds (2.3 kg) of burnished beauty.

Work Surfaces

It's essential to use punches on a poly cutting board; hardwood is too soft and will absorb much of the blow so that the punch doesn't cut through the leather. Punching on a hard surface such as thick glass or marble will ruin the edge on the punch.

To avoid marring the finish on eyelets, set them on a scrap of hardwood. Set rapid rivets on a small, flat piece of thick steel or marble.

Fastening

Fastening methods in these projects range from beading techniques (such as crimping) to sewing- and leather-specific methods.

A bead crimper looks like a pair of pliers; the technique for using it is explained on page 31.

When hand sewing, you can use heavy-duty thread and a large needle, if you've prepunched holes with an awl or another tool. (If you haven't, sew with a glovers needle, which has a triangular-shaped point instead of a round one.) The notions department of your favorite fabric store will sell sewing-machine needles designed specifically for muscling through leather. Remember that unlike with fabric, you can't unpick stitching in leather without leaving a permanent trail of visible holes, so be sure to sew in exactly the right spot.

You must have a specialized rivet setter to set rivets; you'll find it anyplace you buy the hardware. It's a rod with a concave end that prevents the caps from flattening.

In much the same vein, purchase the appropriate eyelet-setting kit wherever you purchase your eyelets.

A snap-setting kit consists of two parts—an anvil in which to cradle the bottom part of the snap, and a rod. Packets of grommets usually include the grommet setter as part of the set.

Miscellaneous Tools

For drawing outlines and making other marks, any permanent marker with a fine point will do the job. You'll need a measuring tool for many of the projects. A metal ruler can serve double duty, both for figuring lengths and for guiding blades during cutting; a tape measure is handy for extensive lengths.

A few tools are needed for only one project. The Channels cuff (page 101) calls for a stitch groover and an edge beveler, but they're not required for any other projects. You'll find these tools wherever leather specialty tools are sold. A knot template makes creating the Knots earrings (page 76) a snap. Look for this in yarn stores, in the notions department of fabric stores, or online.

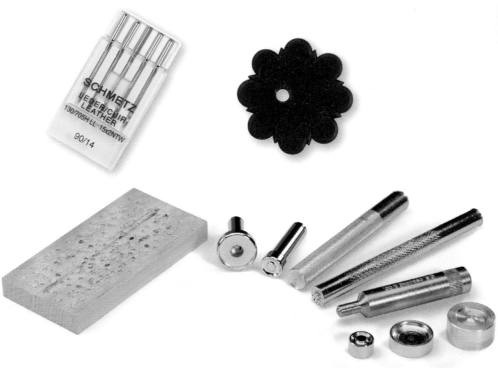

Clockwise from top left: Leather needles for sewing machines; a knot template; an assortment of tools for setting eyelets, snaps, and grommets; a scrap of hardwood

LEATHER TECHNIQUES

Anytime you're trying a new technique or working with a thickness of leather you've never used before, practice on a scrap piece first.

Removing Creases

If your leather has wrinkles or folds due to improper storage, you can get them out with a household iron. Preheat the appliance to 80°F (26.7°C), or the lowest temperature possible. Place a clean, damp (not wet) cloth—one that's been washed so it doesn't contain starches or manufacturing chemicals—over the wrong side of the leather and carefully press it. Don't leave the iron in any one spot for long, and check the creased area frequently so you notice when it's gone and know to stop.

Cutting Leather

As long as you've got sharp blades on your scissors, you'll find it's no harder to cut leather than it is to snip through card stock. The same goes for the blades on rotary cutters, utility knives, and craft knives.

If you need to cut a long straight line in leather, your best bet is to use a bladed tool (such as a craft knife or rotary cutter) guided by a straightedge. For short curves, a craft knife or scissors work equally well.

Sewing

The only hand sewing in this book involves making a knot here and there. Thin, garment-grade leathers—those up to 1.2 millimeters (³⁄₆₄ inch) or 3 ounces—sew easily on a home machine. (Some machines can lurch through heavier weights, but it's really hard on the motor, so avoid it.) Install a leather needle in it, and set the stitch length as long as it will go. A roller foot or a Teflon foot can make the sewing easier, but neither is absolutely necessary. Here's a handy trick: place a sheet of freezer paper on the leather, waxy side up, to help it slide under the presser foot. (Be sure to use freezer paper rather than wax paper, which has wax on both sides; you don't want any wax getting embedded in your leather!) After you've finished stitching, the freezer paper tears off easily.

JOSEPHINE BERGSØE | *Bracelets*

Mink fur, diamonds, keshi pearl, silver, gold
PHOTO BY KRISTIAN GRANQUIST

Punching

To use a rotating punch, start by dialing the desired punch size over the table. Slide the leather into the tool, positioning the spot to be punched under the punch itself. Squeeze the handle, the way you would pliers, until you feel the softness of the leather give way.

When using hollow punches, always work on a poly cutting board (placing it on a solid base) to avoid ruining the cutting edge on the tool. Don't work on a wood block; it's too soft and will simply absorb both the leather and the punch, so the cut will look ragged—if you manage to cut anything at all. The bigger the punch, the heavier the mallet and the greater the force you'll need to use to drive the tool through. Don't ever use a hammer; striking the punch with metal can damage it and dull the cutting edge. (By the way, if you don't want to invest in punches, you can always trace a round shape and cut it out. It won't look as perfect as if it were punched, but it'll do.)

To determine the size of hole to punch for eyelets, rivets, or snaps, follow the manufacturer's directions. If no size is listed, use the smallest hole possible for the hardware to fit through, testing it on a scrap piece of the same leather you plan to use for your project.

Setting Leather Eyelets

These are a cinch to set.

COLLECT

Appropriate size punch

Appropriate size eyelet-setting kit

Scrap of leather or fabric

Scrap of hardwood

Mallet

Gather your kit. Punch a hole in your leather piece the same diameter as the eyelet or slightly smaller, and insert the eyelet from the grain side of the leather. The eyelet shouldn't go all the way through the hole; its lip should catch on the leather ❶.

Flip the leather over so it's grain side down, with the tubular part of the eyelet sticking up through the hole ❷. Put your work on a scrap of leather or fabric to protect the finish on the eyelet, and then on the anvil if one came with the eyelet-setting kit. (If not, use a scrap of hardwood.)

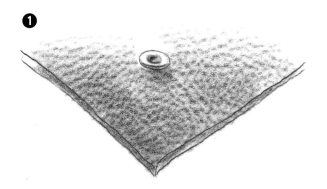

❶

❷

Place the pointed tip of the eyelet setter into the eyelet tube ❸ and tap the setter lightly with a mallet until its sides flatten against the leather. Opened up like that, the metal looks like an asterisk ❹.

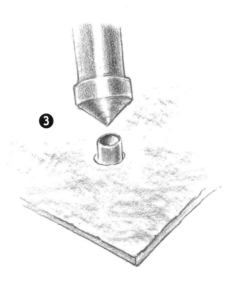

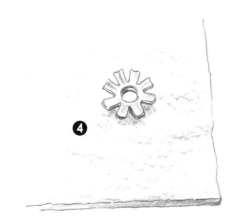

Setting Grommets

Follow the instructions that come with the grommet-setting kit. The grommet part goes on the grain side of the leather, and the washer mounts on the wrong side. Always practice on a scrap first, because it's impossible to take apart a grommet.

Setting Rapid Rivets

Rapid rivets have two halves. The top, which will be visible on the right side of the work, has a slightly domed cap and an external shaft. The other half has a smaller internal shaft ending in a flat head; when mounted, it will be visible on the back side of the leather.

COLLECT

Punch matching diameter of internal shaft of rivet

Poly cutting board (if not using a rotating punch)

Rapid rivet setter

Piece of flat steel or marble

Mallet

Punch holes in the leather pieces you wish to fasten together. Put the bottom half of the rivet on the steel or marble, standing on its head. Slide the holes, with the leather grain side up, onto the shaft ❺. (Slip on the piece of leather that goes on the bottom first, then the one that belongs on top.) For best results, the internal shaft should stick out no more than 3 millimeters (⅛ inch). Otherwise, it has a tendency to bend in the next step, and won't set properly.

Cap the shaft with the top half of the rivet. Place the rivet setter over the cap ❻, and give a sharp blow of the mallet to pound the halves together permanently.

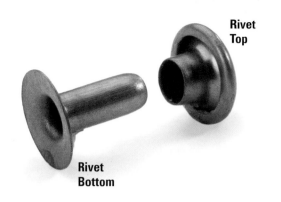

Rivet Top

Rivet Bottom

Setting Snaps

Snaps attach overlapping pieces of leather, with the attaching unit fastened to the leather on the outer part of the overlap. The closure unit gets mounted to the leather resting closest to the body (the part that appears below the overlap).

LEATHER SNAPS

The sturdier type of snap sold for leatherwork has a post, so you'll have to punch a hole to accommodate this. (See page 28 for instructions on setting the prong style of snap, which will work for thinner leathers.)

COLLECT

Hole punch in appropriate size

Flaring tool and die

Mallet

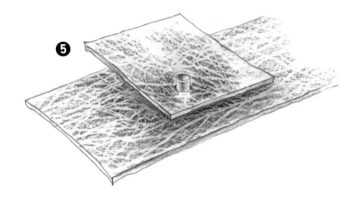

❺

Stud

Socket

Stud post

Capped post

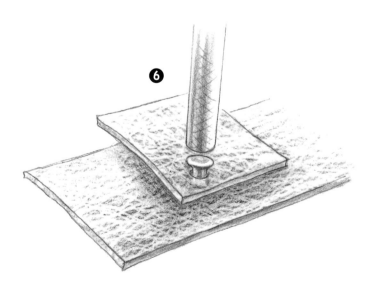

❻

Work on a hard surface. Refer to the photo above for the terminology of the various parts. Set the attachment unit—the front of the snap, comprised of the capped post and the socket—first, making sure you install it on the part of the leather that will be the overlap. Punch a hole in the leather.

Put the die, concave side up, on your work surface and place the capped post in it with the shaft sticking up ❼. Slip the leather over the post, grain side down, and place the socket on the shaft ❽. Put the tip of the flaring tool into the shaft and set the snap with a firm blow of the mallet.

To mount the closure unit to the overlap, first determine its placement in relation to the attachment unit, and punch a hole. Put the stud post in the shallow side of the anvil, shaft up ❾, and slide the leather over it, grain side up. Place the stud onto the shaft ❿. With the tip of the flaring tool held in the shaft, set the unit by again tapping with the mallet.

HEAVY-DUTY FABRIC SNAPS

You can buy these in the notions department of fabric stores; because of the prongs, you won't have to punch a hole.

COLLECT

Scrap of hardwood

Scrap of fabric

Hammer

Pencil topped with eraser

Die and setter from heavy-duty snap-setting kit

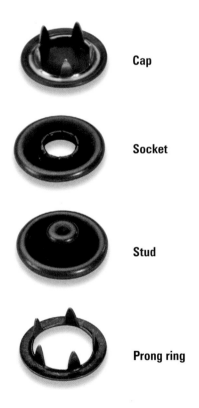

Cap

Socket

Stud

Prong ring

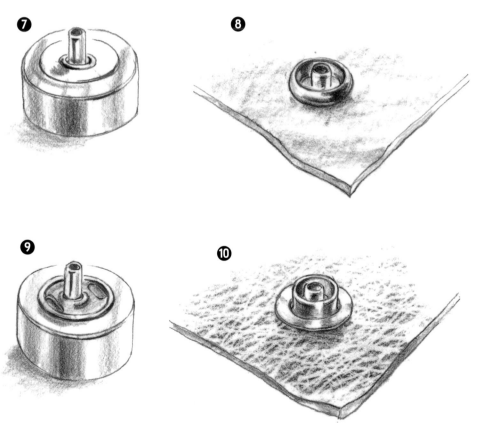

Work on a hard surface. Refer to the photo above for the terminology of the various parts. Set the attachment unit first. Mark its placement on the grain side of the leather. Place the hardwood scrap on your work surface with the leather on it, grain side up. Put the cap at the marked spot, prongs down 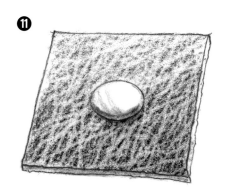. To protect the finish on the cap, put a scrap of fabric over it, then tap lightly with the hammer to drive the prongs through the leather.

Pull the leather off the wood and flip it over; press the pencil eraser over the prongs to push them all completely through the material. Set the die on your work surface, concave side up. Put the cap into the die; the leather will be grain side down, with the prongs peeping through 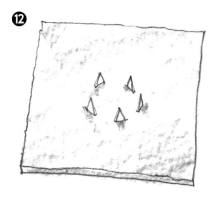. Balance the socket on the prongs; it's impossible to describe which side of the socket faces up, but one fits better then the other, so just try both to determine the correct orientation. Place the setter over the socket 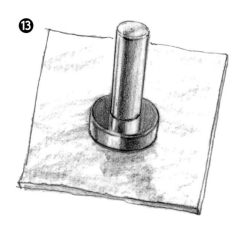 and give a firm blow of the hammer to set the attachment unit.

To set the closure unit, mark the snap placement on the wrong side of the leather. Begin with the hardwood on your work surface, and place the leather on it grain side down. Put the prong ring in the appropriate spot, prongs against the leather . Tap lightly with the hammer to start driving the prongs through the leather, and finish the job with the pencil eraser. Put the fabric on your work surface to protect the finish on the prong ring, place the leather grain side up on it so the prongs face up, and balance the stud on the points. With the setter in place, hammer.

11

12

13

14

Dyeing Vegetable-Tanned Leather

Because vegetable-tanned leather naturally darkens with exposure to light, and because aniline dyes are mostly translucent, leather you've applied color to won't remain the same shade as when you originally dyed or stained it. Do note that areas of leather with flaws, scratches, or tooling will take color differently. Unless advised specifically in the instructions, always dye or stain the leather before cutting out the jewelry components, because leather can shrink as it dries. If achieving a specific, stable shade is important to you, experiment first with the various commercial dyes on a scrap of the same leather you plan to use for your jewelry. After it's made, store your finished jewelry in a lightproof box.

Set up in a well-ventilated area with access to a sink, and cover your work surface with plain paper; don't use newsprint—the ink could transfer to the leather.

Any oils the leather may have absorbed during handling could prevent an even absorption of dyes, so you must first clean the surface with lemon concentrate. Apply lemon juice to a damp (not wet) sponge and wipe the surface of the leather. While you wait one or two minutes, rinse the sponge with clean water and wring it out. Wipe the treated areas of the leather with the clean, damp sponge to neutralize the acid in the lemon. Allow the leather to dry before dyeing. Apply several light coats of stain or dye, rather than a single heavy one, using a swab or piece of clean fabric in a circular motion.

All kinds of effects are possible, particularly if you use multiple colors. Sponged textures, dragging the brush to create a wood-like grain, shading, and combing are just a few. Look for techniques booklets wherever you buy your leather dyes or paints. To protect the colored surface, seal it with a compatible leather finish (many are available), following the manufacturer's instructions.

Preventing Crocking

Loose fibers on suede can fall off during use, and if the dye isn't colorfast, pigment can transfer onto your garments, just by light rubbing during wear—that's called crocking, and you want to avoid it! To prevent it, sandwich one end of the suede strand firmly between a clean, folded washcloth, and pull the strand through to remove any excess dye. Repeat three times to make sure you get it all.

Color Me Beautiful

All but one of the projects in this book started with leather that had already been dyed commercially. The advantage of predyed leather over dyeing your own vegetable-tanned leather is it's less likely to fade over time, it comes in every color of the rainbow (and then some), and the shades can be brighter.

A few manufacturers still use aniline dyes, which are derived from petroleum, but it's now possible to avoid these chemicals with water-based dyes, stains, and paints.

NON-LEATHER TECHNIQUES

The more techniques you have tucked in your bag of tricks, the more variations and possibilities you have for design.

Crimping Beads

Although it's possible to squeeze a crimp bead flat with nothing more than chain-nose pliers, this creates an iffy connection. Use crimping pliers instead for a secure outcome.

Slide the crimp bead onto the wire and into position. Look at the jaws of the crimping pliers, and you'll notice two sets of openings: a U-shaped one closer to the handle, and a circular one nearer the tip **15**. Squeeze the crimp bead in the U-shaped notch first. Then rotate the crimp bead 90° and set it into the round notch. Squeeze to form it into a round tube.

15

MARI ISOPAHKALA | *Rings*
Reindeer fur, silver
PHOTO BY CHIKAKO HARADA

Papercraft Eyelets

All eyelets are set in essentially the same way, so refer to the instructions for setting leather eyelets on page 25.

Prong Snaps

Prong snaps have teeth designed to pierce through fabric, so you don't have to punch a hole; they work just fine on thin leather.

COLLECT

Snap-setting kit

Poly cutting board

Pencil topped with eraser

Mallet

Prong ring

Stud

Socket

Prong ring

Refer to the photo above for the terminology of the various parts. Mount the attachment unit first. Determine the placement of the snap, and mark it on the wrong side of the leather. Place a prong ring on the poly cutting board, with the prongs facing upward. Put the leather on the prongs, grain side down, and press down with the pencil eraser to push the prongs through the leather ⓰. Balance the socket on the prongs ⓱. (Because of its design, it's impossible to describe which side of the socket should face up; just try both sides. One fits better than the other, and you'll feel it immediately.) Put the setter onto the socket ⓲ and hammer firmly with a mallet to set the snap.

To set the closure unit, mark its placement on the leather, then set a prong unit— prongs up—on the poly cutting board. This time, lay the leather over the prongs grain side up and push the prongs through the material with the help of the pencil eraser. Balance the stud on the prongs ⓳. Position the setter over the socket and hammer to set it.

⓰

⓱

⓲

⑲

MICHAELA BINDER | *Bracelet*

Mink fur, silver
PHOTO BY ARTIST

AIKO MACHIDA | *Charms, necklace charm/hair accessory/brooch*

Clockwise from top left, Planet (two); Nebula; Asteroid
(three); Meteor; detail of Nebula as a hair accessory

Cowhide, hand-dyed leather, oxidized silver chain
PHOTOS BY KOJI UDO

Rubber Stamping

You'll get the best results from permanent or solvent-based ink pads recommended for fabric or leather. Some pigments require special procedures, such as heat, for setting. To make sure it will create a sharp image and to check the required drying time, test the rubber stamp and the ink on a scrap of the same leather you're planning to use for your finished item.

Work on a smooth, flat surface. Don't rock the stamp from side to side—this may distort the image. Instead, press down firmly on the stamp with your palms to ensure that all parts of the image make contact with the leather.

Opening Jump Rings

You'll need two sets of chain-nose pliers. Always open jump rings by holding each end with pliers, near the opening; twist one end of the ring toward you and the other end away ❷⓿. If you pull the ends straight apart, it will distort the shape of the ring.

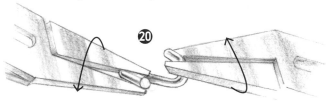

Bead Loops and Wrapped Bead Loops

In this book, a bead loop describes a piece of wire with a bead on it, held there by loops on either side that link to the rest of the jewelry.

To make one, cut 3 inches (7.6 cm) of wire. About ½ inch (1.3 cm) from one end, make a 90° bend with the round-nose pliers ❷①. Hold the wire with longer portion pointing down and the short bent end pointing toward you. Grasp the short end with the pliers, holding the tool so the back of your hand faces you. Keeping the tips stationary, rotate the pliers up and away,

stopping when you've made half a loop and being careful not to unbend the 90° angle ❷❷. Slide the tip of the pliers back along the wire a little and finish making the rest of the loop ❷❸. Cut off any extra wire. Next, slide a bead onto the wire and fashion another loop on the other end of the wire, starting it right next to the bead.

A wrapped bead loop is merely a variation on the bead loop, with wire looped and wrapped on either side of the bead for a more secure connection. Start with a little longer piece of wire to account for the wraps, and make your initial 90° angle ¾ inch (1.9 cm) from the end. Once you've made the loop, don't cut off the extra wire. Instead, position your pliers inside the loop to steady the work and use your other hand to wrap the tail of wire around the base of the loop a few times ❷④, then cut off any excess. Slide on your bead and repeat the process on the other side ❷⑤.

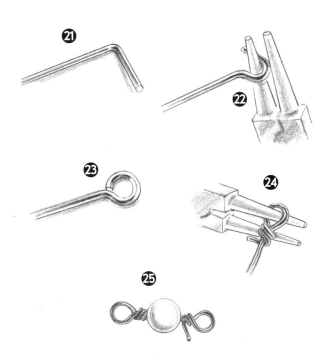

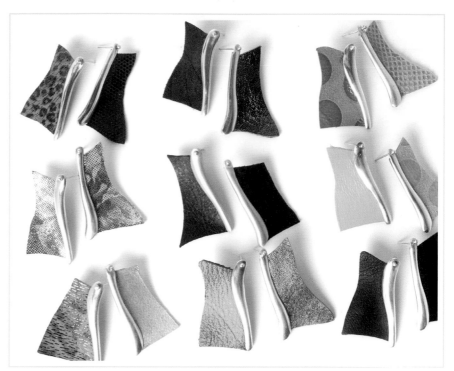

MARINA MOLINELLI WELLS | *Pétalos, earrings*
Cow leather, silver
PHOTO BY ARTIST

ALESSANDRA CALVANI | *Euclide, necklace*
Leather, metal
PHOTO BY GILBERTO MALTINTI

COLLECT

Leather

12 x 12 inches (30.5 x 30.5 cm)
of rose-colored garment-tanned
pig suede
very soft 0.4–0.8 mm/1–2 oz.

Matching thread

2 eyelets, 1/8 inch (3 mm) in diameter

1 1/4 yards (1.1 m) of 6-pound braided
beading thread

9 inches (22.9 cm) of brass chain

7 to 11 brass filigree beads, 14 mm

Brass lobster clasp

Pen

Ruler

Scalloping shears

Sewing machine with leather needle

Rotary punch

Eyelet-setting tool

Scissors

Needle

Wire cutters

Flat-nose pliers

MAKE

1 Make a long strip of suede by drawing two parallel lines 1¼ inches (3.2 cm) apart on the wrong side of the material. Cut along the lines with the scalloping shears, making sure the scallops face outward on either edge. Repeat until you've cut enough strips to achieve a combined length of 80 inches (2 m).

2 Sew the strips into one long strip with lapped seams. To do so, place one strip grain side up. Put another strip over it, also with the grain facing up, overlapping the ends by 1 inch (2.5 cm). Stitch down the center of the overlap, then trim closc to the seam on both the right side and the wrong side.

3 Lay the strip of suede flat and horizontal on a work surface. Working from its left end, mark a point that's centered along the width of the strip, close to the edge.

4 Draw a point ¼ inch (6 mm) to the right of the first one. Draw another point ⅝ inch (1.6 cm) to the right of the second one. Repeat along the length of the entire strip, alternating the measurements ❶. Set the rotary punch to make the smallest hole possible, and punch holes at every point.

Texture, texture, texture. In a choker fit for a queen, the softest suede, tightly gathered, frames filigree orbs.

❶

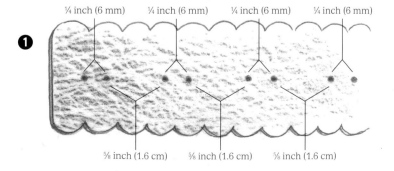

¼ inch (6 mm)   ¼ inch (6 mm)   ¼ inch (6 mm)   ¼ inch (6 mm)

⅝ inch (1.6 cm)   ⅝ inch (1.6 cm)   ⅝ inch (1.6 cm)

Design by Nathalie Mornu

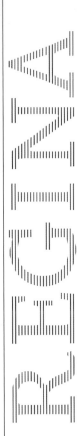

5 Set one eyelet in the leftmost pair of holes so that it catches the wrong sides, making a sort of hem. Trim the edge into a curve **❷**.

6 Thread the needle with the beading thread and double it. Cut a 6-inch (15.2 cm) piece of chain and tie the end of the thread to an end link. Run the needle through the right side of the eyelet.

7 You'll weave the thread through the holes in the strip as follows: the thread shows on the right side of the suede between the ¼-inch (6 mm) holes **❸**. It shows on the wrong side of the suede between the ⅝-inch (1.6 cm) holes.

❷

Begin by picking up five ruffles as counted from the right side of the suede, then pass through a filigree bead.

8 Pick up five more ruffles, then add another bead. As you weave, push the strip along the thread to create tight ruffles, adjusting both the ruffles and the beads so they're even. Repeat until all the beads have been strung, or until you've achieved the desired length. (Keep checking the length as you work until the ruffled strip is 2 inches [5.1 cm] short of reaching all the way around your neck.) Next, pick up only four more ruffles. Don't cut the thread.

9 In the next pair of holes, mount an eyelet in the way described in step 5. Trim off any extra strip. Run the needle and thread through the back of the eyelet. Set aside momentarily.

10 Attach the lobster clasp to the remaining chain. Trim the chain so it's 1 inch (2.5 cm) long.

11 Cut the needle off the thread, being sure to leave an 8-inch (20.3 cm) tail. Tie the thread to the chain cut in the previous step (not the end with the clasp on it, obviously), making sure you pull the final set of ruffles tight as you make the knot.

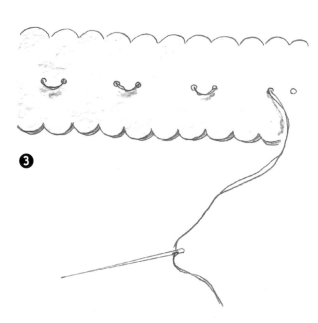

❸

You're chic, sophisticated, and made to dance the Charleston—yet somehow the stars misaligned and you were born a century too late. No matter. Throw on this necklace and turn up the music.

Design by Trilby Hainstock

COLLECT

Leather

2 7/8 yards (2.6 m) of round white leather cord semifirm 2 mm

1 1/2 yards (1.4 m) of round black leather cord semifirm 2 mm

8 rectangular gold-finish multistrand spacers, 3.5 x 15 mm (to fit 6 cords)

2 rectangular gold-finish multistrand spacers, 3.5 x 25 mm (to fit 12 cords)

2 gold-finish head pins

2 gold-finish bead caps

2 gold-finish jump rings

Gold-finish lobster clasp

Clear-drying two-part epoxy

Ruler

Scissors

Jewelry pliers with one flat and one round jaw

Poly cutting board

Craft knife

Round-nose pliers

Wire snips

MAKE

1 Measure and cut the leather cords into pieces 12⅝ inches (32 cm) long, to end up with eight white ones and four black ones.

2 String two black cords and four white ones through one of the smaller spacers, and arrange them flat on a work surface, with the black cords on the outsides. Arrange the cords so all the tips line up. Position the spacer 3¾ inches (9.5 cm) from one of the ends and use jewelry pliers to squeeze the spacer closed against the cords so it can't slide along them. Slip on a second spacer, place it right beside the first, and squeeze it closed so it won't slide.

3 Using the remaining cords, repeat step 2.

4 Working with both sets of cords, on the sides where the cords extend 3½ inches (8.9 cm) or so beyond the paired spacers, string on a long spacer. Form gentle outward curves for the neck with both sets of cords, and position the long spacer 2 inches (5.1 cm) away from the already placed spacers. Make sure the closed spacers are level with each other, then squeeze the long spacer closed to hold it in place. String on the other long spacer, snug it against the first, and squeeze it closed **❶**.

5 Place the work on the poly cutting board, hold the 12 cords down firmly, side by side, and cut a symmetrical V-shaped point at the end with a craft knife.

6 Working from the end that isn't pointed, string a small spacer onto one of the sets of cords. Position it 2½ inches (6.4 cm) from the pair of spacers mounted in step 2, and curve the cords gently back inward. Squeeze it closed.

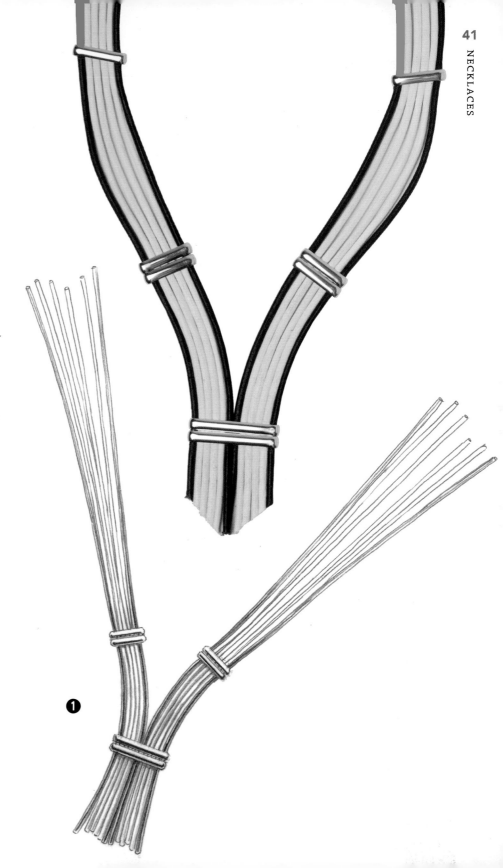

Making sure you maintain the curvature of the cords, attach a small spacer 2¼ inches (5.7 cm) from the previous one.

7 Repeat step 6 on the other set of cords.

8 Making sure you preserve the curvature of the cords, cut the tips off flush on both sets, 2⅛ inches (5.4 cm) from the most recently mounted spacers. Set aside.

9 Push a head pin through the hole in a bead cap, with the head inside the cap. Use the round-nose pliers to make a loop as close as possible to the cap, and snip off any excess wire. Repeat with the other head pin and bead cap.

10 Attach a jump ring to each of the loops made in the previous step, catching the lobster clasp in one of them.

11 Mix up a small quantity of epoxy according to the manufacturer's instructions. Apply some to the very tips of one set of cords to glue them to each other. Do the same to the other set of cords. Dab epoxy inside both of the bead caps and insert one set of cords into each. Allow to dry completely.

❶

COLLECT

Leather

15 yards (13.7 m)* of red garment-tanned pig suede lacing, ⅛ inch (3 mm) wide very soft 0.4–0.8 mm/1–2 oz.

44 inches (1.1 m) of ¼-inch (6 mm) round cord, in color matching the suede lacing

6 inches (15.2 cm) of 22-gauge half-hard round sterling silver wire

2 sterling silver cones, ½ inch (1.3 cm) long

2 sterling silver beads, 4 mm

2 soldered-closed jump rings, 5.3 mm

1 S-shaped sterling silver hook clasp

Scissors

Measuring tape

Clean white terrycloth washcloth

6 plastic zip-top bags, 2 x 2 inches (5.1 x 5.1 cm)

Epoxy

Thread

Wire cutters

Pliers

Jeweler's cement

Round-nose pliers

*You may need more than 15 yards; see step 1 for an explanation.

MAKE

1 Cut the suede lacing into six strands, each 90 inches (2.3 m) long. As you measure, inspect the lacing for splices. No strand should contain a splice, so if you come across one, discard the strand and replace it with another.

2 Pull the suede strands through the washcloth to prevent crocking (page 30). Roll each strand into a small ball and place it inside its own sandwich bag, with about 5 inches (12.7 cm) of lace extending from the top of the bag. Close the bags as much as possible.

3 On one end of the round cord, apply a light coat of glue to the first ¼ inch (6 mm) of material. Arrange the tips of the suede strands evenly around the cord, pressing each strand so it adheres to the cord. Wrap and tie thread around the suede-wrapped cord ¼ inch (6 mm) from the end. Position the bags containing the strands so three are on the left of the cord—at the left back, left side, and left front—and three are on the right—at the right front, right side, and right back positions ❶. In the illustration, these have been labeled 1 through 6, respectively. Mark your bags with the same numbers to help you keep them straight.

An extra-long necklace is so versatile. Wear it as a single strand, double it, wrap it around the neck three times—you can even bind your wrist with it.

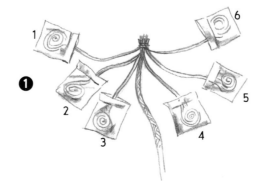

❶

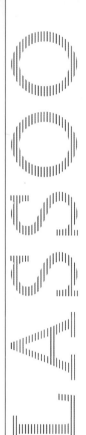

4 The braiding isn't immediately intuitive; don't try to understand what you're doing, just follow the instructions to the letter and everything will work. Begin by flipping the left front strand (labeled 3) over the cord, and crossing over it with the original right front strand (labeled 4). Your work should look like ❷.

5 Bring the right back strand (labeled 6) around the back of the cord and over the left back strand (labeled 1), under the left side strand (labeled 2), and over the left front strand, bringing the strand you've just woven to the right of the cord, where it now becomes the right front strand. Rotate the cord slightly so that it's clear which position each strand occupies; your work should look like ❸. After each braiding pass, you should always end with three strands to the right of the core cord and three strands to the left.

6 Bring the left back strand around the back and over the right back strand, under the right side strand, and over the right front strand, ending with the strand you've just woven to the left of the cord, where it now becomes the left front strand ❹. Rotate the cord slightly so that it's clear which position each strand occupies.

7 Repeat steps 5 and 6; you'll notice a diagonal basketweave pattern forming. Pretty cool, huh? Continue alternating steps 5 and 6 until the entire length of the cord is covered in a suede braid. After each pass, make sure none of the strands has twisted or folded and check that all strands are in the correct position. As you go, gently tighten the braiding, using your thumbnail to ease the strands into place. (Don't tug—breakage could occur.) When necessary, pull a manageable length of suede from each bag as the work progresses.

8 At the end of the cord, trim any excess suede so that all ends are even with the end of the cord. Glue each suede strand to the core, maintaining its position so it doesn't pull or twist, and allow the glue to dry. Wrap and tie thread around the suede-wrapped cord, about ¼ inch (6 mm) from the end.

9 Cut the wire into two equal lengths.

10 Use the pliers to make a 90° bend at the center point of one of the wires. Tuck the thread-wrapped area of one end of the cord into the bend in the wire, and wrap half of the wire around the cord, allowing the other end of the wire to extend beyond the cord ❺.

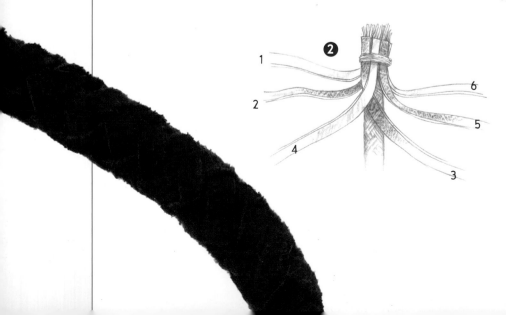

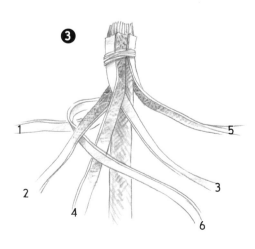

11 Apply a light coat of jeweler's cement to the inside of a cone and to the entire wire-wrapped area of the cord. Slip the larger opening of the cone over the wire, pull the cone against the end of the cord, and hold it in place for 10 minutes to allow the bonding to take place.

12 Slip a bead onto the wire. Using round-nose pliers, make a wrapped loop (page 34) above the bead, catching a jump ring in the loop.

13 Repeat steps 10 to 12 on the other end of the braid-covered cord. Slide one side of the S-shaped clasp onto either one of the jump rings and squeeze the clasp so the two won't come apart.

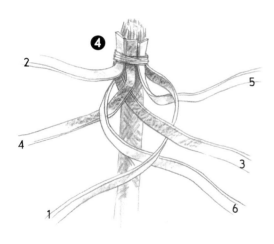

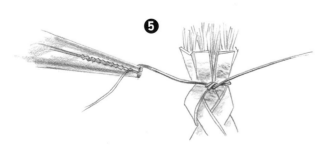

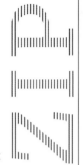

COLLECT

Leather

3 x 30 inches (7.6 x 76.2 cm) of crocodile-embossed patent (or other top-finished, garment-tanned) leather soft 0.4–0.8 mm/1–2 oz.

1 black zipper with silver teeth, 22 inches (55.9 cm) long

Thread to match leather

Measuring tape

Pen

Cutting mat

Rotary cutter

Yardstick

Shears

Sewing machine with zipper foot and leather needle

MAKE

1 Close the zipper; with a measuring tape, measure from the slider, or pull, to the bottom stop. On the wrong side of the leather, mark the eventual placement of the zipper by drawing a line exactly that length, centered between both sides and both ends.

2 Using the cutting mat, the rotary cutter, and the yardstick, carefully slit along the line; *do not* cut beyond it.

3 Put the zipper right side up on your worktable. Place the leather over the zipper, grain side up, with the ends of the slit lined up with the zipper's slider and bottom stop. Trim the leather with shears to allow the slider to fit through. Remove the zipper. Along the rest of the slit, trim ⅛ inch (3 mm) off both sides.

4 Install a zipper foot and a leather needle on the sewing machine. Place the leather wrong side up and put the zipper over it, its slider and bottom stop lined up with the ends of the slit ❶. Attach the zipper to the leather by machine stitching with matching thread along the edges of the slit, close to the zipper teeth. The leather may stretch a little; to accommodate that, you should sew in the same direction on both sides of the zipper. Leave the zipper foot on the machine.

5 Place the short leather grain sides together, forming a large ring, and stitch them, using a ⅛-inch (3 mm) seam allowance.

6 On one side of the zipper, fold the long side of the leather up to meet the back of the zipper, lining up the straight edge of the leather against the teeth. Alongside only the zipper, stitch the leather down through all layers to encase the zipper tape. Do the same on the other side of the zipper tape ❷. (To give a better understanding of the construction, some of the elements in the illustration haven't been included.)

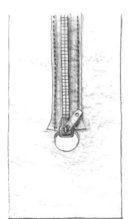

❶

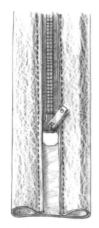

❷

Borrowing loosely from bomber jackets, with their industrial zippers, this neckwear features an unexpected bit of hardware. Wear it open or closed.

Design by Joan K. Morris

COLLECT

Leather

24 x 24 inches (61 x 61 cm) of metallic (or other top-finished) garment-tanned lambskin soft 0.4–0.8 mm/1–2 oz.

Scrap of card stock

80 antique eyelets, ⅛ inch (3 mm) in diameter

Scissors

Scalloping scissors

Pedicure scissors

Iron

Marker

Hole punch

Eyelet-setting kit

MAKE

1 Copy the templates on page 126 and transfer them onto card stock to make them sturdier. Cut them out with scissors.

2 Trace the template labeled Center onto the lambskin 40 times. Cut them out, using scalloping scissors to cut the exterior curve, and using the pedicure scissors to cut the tight interior curve as well as the straight lines.

3 Trace the template labeled End onto the lambskin. Flip the template over, and trace it again. Cut both end pieces out, again using the scalloping scissors on the exterior curve and the nail scissors for the tight interior curve and straight line. Press all the leather pieces (page 24) to remove any creases.

ZHORDA DISCO

Here's a corkscrew to wrap around your neck, to flounce with, to twirl, to twist around your arm. Work it!

Design by Nathalie Mornu

4 Here's how to achieve the corkscrew appearance of the assembled boa.

a: Place one of the end pieces, grain side down, on the table, referring to ❶ for orientation. Still referring to ❶, lay a center piece over it, also grain side down, with a ¼-inch (6 mm) overlap; mark the placement of three holes.

b: Punch holes where marked ❷.

c: Insert and set an eyelet in each hole (page 25) ❸.

d: Place a center piece over the previous two, with a ¼-inch (6 mm) overlap as shown in ❹, and mark three holes. Set eyelets in the holes. Repeat **a** through **d** using only center pieces until all have been assembled.

5 Attach the remaining end piece in the established manner.

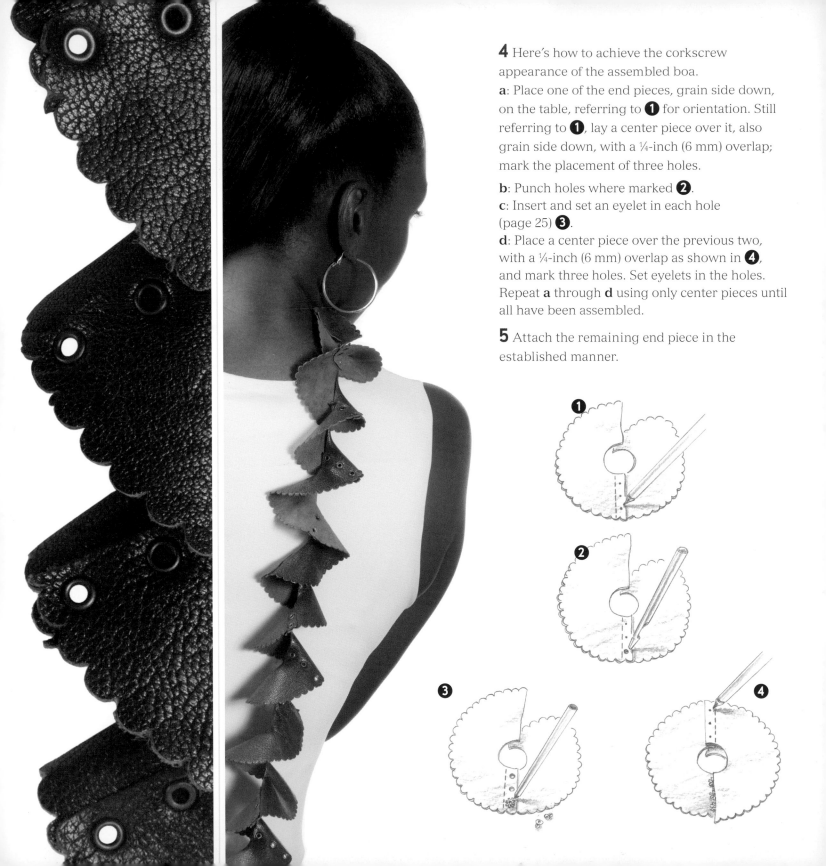

CIRQUE

In leather, velvet, and organza, people will mistake you for an artiste.

Design by Joan K. Morris

Leather

10 x 10 inches (25.4 x 25.4 cm) of orange garment-tanned leather soft 0.8–1.2 mm/2–3 oz., for bottom layer

10 x 10 inches (25.4 x 25.4 cm) of burgundy garment-tanned leather soft 0.8–1.2 mm/2–3 oz., for third layer

3 x 20 inches (7.6 x 50.8 cm) of rust garment-tanned suede very soft 0.8–1.2 mm/2–3 oz., for top layer

3 inches (7.6 cm) of gray organza, 44 inches (1.1 m) wide, for fourth layer

2 inches (5.1 cm) of gold velvet, 44 inches (1.1 m) wide, for second layer

Orange thread

30 inches (76.2 cm) of antique silver chain

1 antique silver clasp

Scissors

Shears

Sewing machine

Needle-nose pliers

❶

1 Enlarge both templates on page 127 and cut them out with scissors. Note that this necklace consists of five layers; they'll be referred to as the top, second, third, fourth, and bottom layers, with "second" meaning second from the top.

2 Trace the template for the bottom layer of the necklace onto the grain side of the orange leather and cut it out with shears. Trace the template for the third layer onto the grain side of the burgundy leather and cut it out. Set both aside.

3 To create the fourth layer, fold the organza in half lengthwise. Set the sewing machine for the longest stitch possible and use orange thread to machine baste two parallel rows of stitching close to the fold, leaving the ends of the threads long. At one end of the stitching, knot the bottom—or bobbin—threads to each other. From the other end of stitching, pull gently on the bobbin threads to gather the organza until it's 20 inches (50.8 cm) long. Knot the threads and distribute the gathers evenly.

4 The necklace is assembled from the bottom up. Machine stitch the gathered organza to the bottom piece of leather, wrong side up, with the raw edges of the fabric parallel to and ¼ inch (6 mm) away from the lower edge of the leather **❶**. **Note**: You should stitch over the outer basting line on the organza.

5 Stack the leather cut to serve as the third layer, wrong side up, on the organza, with the lower edge of the leather parallel to and ¼ inch (6 mm) away from the raw edge of the fabric. Stitch as close as possible along the upper edge of the leather.

6 To make the second layer, begin by sewing two parallel rows of basting stitches along one of the long edges of the velvet. Gather the fabric, as described in step 3, until it's 18 inches (45.7 cm) long. Stack the velvet on the third layer, parallel to and ¼ inch (6 mm) away from the lower edge of the leather. Stitch everything together along the outer basting line on the velvet. Set aside.

7 Place the chain along one long edge of the rectangle of suede with 10 inches (25.4 cm) extending on each side. Fold the edge over the chain ¾ inch (1.9 cm) and stitch near the edge, encasing the chain as you do ❷.

8 Gather the suede along the length of chain until it's the same length as the upper, concave curve of the four stitched-together pieces. Stack the suede atop the other pieces, matching the fold of the suede casing to the upper edge of the bottom layer. Stitch along the stitching line used to encase the chain.

9 Trim the unstitched side of the suede into a curve that's ¼ to ½ inch (6 mm to 1.3 cm) from the raw edge of the velvet. Round the edge where the chain exits from the casing. Use needle-nose pliers to attach the clasp to one end of the chain.

❷

COLLECT

Leather

4 x 10 inches (10.2 x 25.4 cm) of dyed garment-tanned leather slightly firm 0.8–1.2 mm/2–3 oz.

30 rapid rivets, $3/8$ inch (1 cm) diameter

Nail polish in color matching the leather

4 large punches ranging from $3/4$ to $1 3/4$ inches (1.9 to 4.4 cm)*

Mallet

Punches in 2 sizes:
- $1/8$ inch (3 mm)
- $3/16$ inch (5 mm)

Rivet setter

Pedicure scissors

Plastic cutting board

*See page 25 for alternative.

MAKE

1 Punch or cut between 25 and 40 circles in four different sizes, making roughly the same quantity of each.

2 Arrange the circles in a line 16 inches (40.6 cm) long, or as long as needed to fit the intended wearer, making sure the circles overlap.

3 Starting from one end, use the $1/8$-inch (3 mm) punch to make a hole in the first pair (or trio) of circles; rivet them together in such a way that the circles can pivot but that the connection isn't floppy. Move to the next set to attach and repeat. Proceed in this manner to attach all the circles together in a long strip. As you near the end, check the length by trying on the necklace; adjust as necessary.

4 At one end of the strip, punch a hole in which to mount a rivet that will serve as the fastening mechanism. The rivet should fit loosely. To achieve this, cut two or three small scraps of leather with pedicure scissors and punch a $3/16$-inch (5 mm) hole in each. Put the rivet base on the cutting board, thread the punched scraps onto it, then thread the necklace end, right side up. Set the rivet head. Flip the strip over and cut away the scrap pieces of leather.

5 Paint the head of the rivet meant to serve as a fastening mechanism with nail polish to help identify it later when you're wearing the necklace and want to remove it. Allow the polish to dry completely.

6 At the opposite end of the necklace, make the fastening hole by punching a $3/16$-inch (5 mm) hole and cutting a $1/8$-inch (3 mm) notch in it **1**.

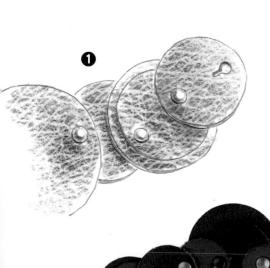

Painting the fastening rivet with nail polish makes it easy to identify.

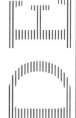

In this straightforward necklace, a sequence of punched circles pivots on rivets. An ingeniously simple closure mechanism blends in with the rest of the design.

Design by Nathalie Mornu

COLLECT

Leather

6 x 13 inches (15.2 x 33 cm) of
gray garment-tanned deerskin
(or other suede)
soft 0.8–1.2 mm/2–3 oz.

18 to 24 inches (45.7 to 61 cm) of
garment-tanned deerskin
(or other suede) lacing
very soft 0.8–1.2 mm/2–3 oz.

All-purpose sewing thread, gray

Jasper focal bead, drilled,
flat $^{13}/_{16}$ x $^{7}/_{8}$ inch (3 x 2.2 cm)

Cranberry seed beads, size 11/0

Gray seed beads, size 11/0

Silver seed beads, size 6/0

Kevlar or cotton beading thread

6 silver grommets, $^{1}/_{4}$ inch (6 mm)

Craft scissors

Shears

Ballpoint pen

Craft glue

Size 10 beading needles

Needle-nose pliers

Sewing machine with leather needle
and zipper foot

$^{1}/_{8}$-inch (3 mm) punch

Grommet-setting kit

MAKE

1 Enlarge the template on page 124 and cut it out with craft scissors.

2 With shears, cut two pieces of leather, each 3 x 13 inches (7.6 x 33 cm). Set one piece aside and transfer the template onto the other by tracing around the template with pen, making sure you leave at least ¼ inch (6 mm) of space around the edge. Don't transfer the grommet placement.

3 On the grain side of the leather, locate the center of the choker and use a dab of glue to attach the focal bead to that spot. Thread a beading needle with about 24 inches (61 cm) of beading thread, double it, and tie a knot at the end. Once the glue is dry, stitch the stone to the leather with two or three passes of the needle. (Depending on the thickness of the leather, you may need to use a pair of pliers to pull the needle through.) Tie off on the wrong side of the leather.

4 Sew a single row of cranberry seed beads that completely encircles the focal bead, working as follows. Bring the needle up through the leather, near the edge of the focal bead. Load the needle with between one and three seed beads, then poke the needle back through the leather a few millimeters away, working along the edge of the centerpiece bead. Bring the needle back up through the leather some distance away from where it was last inserted, load the needle with enough beads to fill the space, and reinsert the needle at the end of the previous row of beadwork.

Like mist, the deerskin in this choker is incredibly soft against the tender skin of the neck. Use it as a canvas for your beadworking skills.

Design by **Sara McCormick**

5 Expand on the beaded motif by adding a fringe of beads that surrounds the row attached in the previous step, working as follows. Bring the needle up in the desired location. Load it with three gray beads, one larger silver bead, and one cranberry bead, in that order. Thread the needle back through the strung beads, skipping the cranberry bead but going through the silver and gray ones. Then insert the needle back into the leather in the same location and pull it tight ❶. Bring the needle back up nearby, and repeat the process. Work around the focal bead in this manner 2 until it's completely surrounded by a row of fringe ❷. Make sure all the beadwork is secure, and tie off.

6 Use craft glue to attach the piece of leather set aside earlier to the beaded piece, wrong sides together. This will cover the threads from the beadwork. Allow to dry.

7 Thread the sewing machine and mount a leather needle and a zipper foot on it. (The special foot allows the beadwork to pass closer to the needle during sewing.) Working slowly, sew all around, ⅛ inch (3 mm) inside the template outline.

8 Using a beading needle and pliers, secure the loose ends of the sewing thread between the two layers of leather. Trim away the excess leather around the edges of the choker, just inside the outline.

9 Using the template as a guide, mark the grommet placement on both ends of the choker, and set the grommets using the punch and grommet-setting kit.

10 Run the deerskin lacing through the grommets loosely, and tighten it for wear.

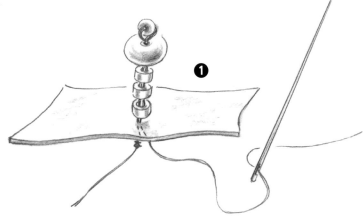

❶

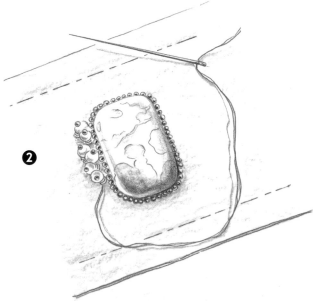

❷

Those catty girls. Their eyes appraise you with envy. The whispers start. What are they saying? It can't be nice.

GOSSIP

Design by Nathalie Mornu

Leather

14 feet (4.3 m) of garment-tanned
suede lacing in lavender
very soft 1.2–1.6 mm/3–4 oz.

14 feet (4.3 m) of garment-tanned
suede lacing in purple
very soft 1.2–1.6 mm/3–4 oz.

Fishing line

4 antique brass closed rings, $3/8$ inch
(1 cm) diameter

7 antique brass eye pins, 2 inches
(5.1 cm) long

2 oval antique brass filigree beads,
$1/2$ inch (1.3 cm) long

38 inches (96.5 cm) of
antique brass chain

6 antique brass jump rings, $5/8$ inch
(1.6 cm) diameter

1 filigree star, 1 $1/4$ inches
(3.2 cm) across

5 filigree tubes, $1/2$ inch (1.3 cm) long

Washcloth

Scissors

Measuring tape

Round-nose pliers

Wire cutters

Chain-nose pliers

1 Pull the suede strands through the washcloth to prevent crocking (page 30). Cut 80 pieces of lacing 4 inches (10.2 cm) long—half of them in one color, and half in the other.

2 Cut a piece of fishing line 24 inches (61 cm) long. Double it, catching a closed ring in a loop at the center.

3 Tie a 4-inch (10.2 cm) piece of lacing of either color around the doubled line, using just a single knot and keeping the tails equal in length. Slide the knot against the closed ring. Using a 4-inch (10.2 cm) piece of lacing in the other color, tie it around the line with a single knot and with tails of the same length, and slide it snugly against the previous knotted piece. Continue in this manner, alternating colors, until you've tied on a total of 35 pieces of lacing. Tie the two protruding tails of line together, catching a closed loop in them so that it rests against the last knotted piece of lacing. Tie the line a few more times to secure the knot, and snip off any excess. You should end up with a length of knotted fringe with closed rings attached at both ends. Set aside.

4 Repeat steps 2 and 3, but knot 45 pieces of lacing on the line. Set aside.

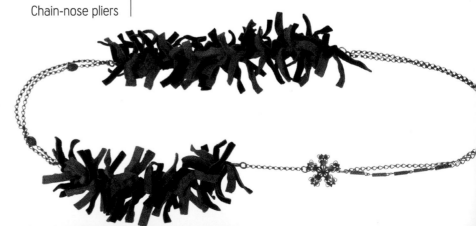

5 Steps 5, 6, and 7 explain how to make the doubled chains hanging at the bottom of the necklace, and how to attach them to the knotted fringe. Use an eye pin and an oval bead to make a wrapped bead loop using the round-nose pliers (page 34). With wire cutters, cut a piece of chain 7 inches (17.8 cm) long. Randomly cut it in two, anywhere along its length, and reattach the pieces by inserting the looped bead in between. Set aside.

6 Make another wrapped bead loop with an oval bead on it. Cut another piece of chain, but make it 7 ½ inches (19 cm) this time. Randomly cut it into two pieces, and use the looped bead to reattach them.

7 Place the two pieces of chain embellished with looped beads side by side and parallel. Open a jump ring (page 34) and catch one pair of the chain ends in it; then slip on one of the closed rings at the end of a length of knotted fringe, and close the jump ring. Use another jump ring to attach the opposite ends of the chains to one of the closed loops at the end of the other length of fringe ❶.

8 The rest of the instructions describe how to make the chains that loop around the neck. Cut a piece of chain 2 inches (5.1 cm) long. Attach it with a jump ring to the free end of the shorter length of fringe. Attach a jump ring to the free end of the 2-inch (5.1 cm) chain; before closing the ring, catch one arm of the filigree star in it.

9 Cut a piece of chain 12 inches (30.5 cm) long. Set it aside.

10 Make five wrapped loops with the filigree tubes and brass eye pins and assemble them in turn to each other. Attach the remaining chain to one end. Lay this chain and the one cut in step 9 side by side and compare them. Cut the longer one so they're exactly the same length.

11 Use a jump ring to attach the end of the chain with the filigree tubes to the arm of the filigree star that's opposite the one with a chain already attached. Before closing the jump ring, add one end of the chain cut in step 9.

12 Using a jump ring, attach the free ends of both chains to the free end of the longer length of fringe.

❶

COLLECT

Leather

8 x 8 inches (20.3 x 20.3 cm)
of off-white top-finish
vegetable-tanned cowhide
firm 0.8–1.2 mm/2–3 oz.

30 inches (76.2 cm) of black satin
rat tail cord

Card stock

Leather cement

Scissors

Pen

Shears

1 knitting needle, size 0/2mm

Black permanent marker

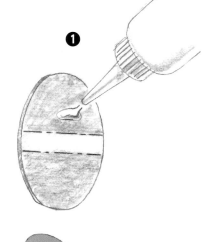

❶

MAKE

1 Copy the templates on page 125, transfer them onto card stock, and cut them out with scissors. Trace them onto the leather with a pen and cut them out with shears, making the quantities listed on the templates.

2 Apply cement to the wrong side of A, leaving a band down the center with no glue on it ❶. Immediately wrap it around the knitting needle, grain side out, as shown in ❷, and allow it to dry completely. Pull it gently off the needle.

3 Repeat step 2 to all B, C, and D pieces.

4 String A onto the rat tail cord. Center it on the rat tail, and tie a knot on each side. String a B on one side of A. Tie a knot to hold it in place. Repeat on the other side of A.

5 String a C next to a B, and tie a knot to hold it on. String the other C next to the other B and tie a knot.

6 String a D next to a C. Tie a knot, then string another D beside it. Tie a knot. Repeat on the other end of the strand.

7 Apply cement to two E pieces and sandwich one end of the rat tail cord between them. Repeat on the other end of the rat tail. Allow to dry completely.

8 Using the permanent marker, carefully draw over the exposed edges of the leather to give a finished appearance.

❷

Oftentimes, simplicity packs a whole lot of punch. Cut, fold, and glue to make leather beads, then string them on a cord.

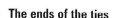

The ends of the ties

Design by Isabelle Azaïs

COLLECT

Leather

1 x 4 inches (2.5 x 10.2 cm) of purple top-finished calf (or other leather) slightly firm 0.8–1.2 mm/2–3 oz.

1 x 4 inches (2.5 x 10.2 cm) of brown top-finished calf (or other leather) slightly firm 0.8–1.2 mm/2–3 oz.

4 antique-brass head pins, 1 1/2 inches (3.8 cm)

4 antique-brass bead cones, 7 x 10 mm

3 1/8 inches (8 cm) of 21-gauge antique-brass wire

2 antique-brass metal beads, 14 mm long

2 glass beads, 9 mm long

2 small antique-brass bead caps, 6 mm in diameter

2 antique-brass ear wires

Scissors

Pen

Poly cutting board

Craft knife

Ruler with metric markings

Cyanoacrylate glue

Round-nose pliers

Wire cutters

MAKE

1 Copy the templates on page 128 and cut them along their outlines only.

2 To make the longer tassels, trace the appropriate template twice onto the purple leather. To cut the fringed area, place the leather on the cutting board and use a craft knife to make parallel slices 3 mm wide, referring to their placement on the template. Be sure not to cut all the way to the opposite side.

3 Place one of the rectangular strips wrong side up on your work surface. Place a head pin on the end of it ❶. (The head should be 7 mm from the long edge.) Roll the leather around the head pin. As you approach the end, place a spot of glue on the upper corner ❷. Finish rolling over the glue and press, holding the roll together for the amount of time recommended by the manufacturer, until the pieces bond. Repeat with the other rectangular strip and a second head pin.

Turn leather fringe on its head by rolling it up. Filigree bead caps top off the little leather tassels.

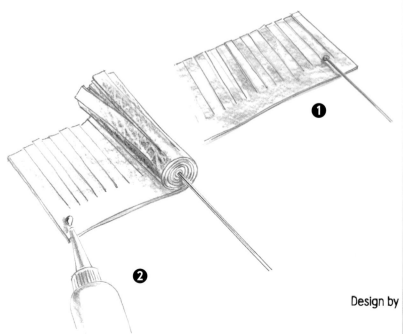

Design by **Delphine Muller**

4 To make the shorter tassels, use the brown leather and the appropriate template, and repeat steps 2 (the parallel cuts for the fringe should be 4 mm wide) and 3.

5 Thread one bead cone onto each head pin, pulling the wire to wedge the tassel tightly inside. Near each cone, make a loop with round-nose pliers (page 34) and cut off any excess wire with wire cutters. Set aside.

6 Cut the 21-gauge wire in half. Set one piece aside.

7 Fashion a loop at one end of the wire; thread on a metal bead, a glass bead, and a bead cap. Make a loop to hold the beads on, cutting off any extra wire.

8 Open the most recent loop made—the one closest to the bead cap—slide the loops of a short tassel and a long tassel on it, and close it. Open the loop of an ear wire, catch the loop next to the wire bead on it, and then close it.

9 With the remaining piece of wire, repeat steps 7 and 8 to make the other earring.

JUDITH PLUCKER | *Rings*

Interchangeable mink-fur inlays, silver
PHOTO BY ARTIST

POM

Clean, spare lines combine with soft fur in a sleek, modern design. All the components are commercial: you need no metalworking skills whatsoever.

Design by Eleanore Macnish

POMPOM

Fur

3 x 3 inches (7.6 x 7.6 cm) of mink

Thread or fishing line

4 sterling silver bead caps, shallow formed and 1/2 inch (1.3 cm) in diameter

2 sterling silver ballpoint head pins, 2 1/4 inches (5.7 cm) long

2 sterling silver crimp beads

Scissors

Ruler

Needle

Needle file or any long, sharp tool

Flat-nose pliers

Ballpoint pen

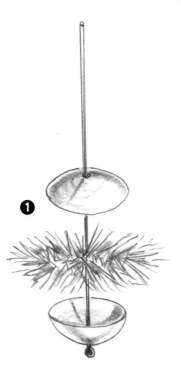

MAKE

1 Cut two pieces of mink from the wrong side, each ¾ x 2 inches (1.9 x 5.1 cm).

2 Thread the needle and make a knot, leaving a long tail. Starting from the wrong side of one corner, insert your needle and use long basting stitches to hand sew along all four edges of one of the rectangles. Make sure that for the final stitch the needle exits on the interior of the hide, not the fur side. Tie a loose double knot in the thread, then gently pull. The edges should ruffle up and produce a pompon shape. Tie another knot and trim the thread ends. Repeat with the second piece of mink.

3 Slide a bead cap onto a head pin, concave side up.

4 Gently work a sharp, narrow tool—such as a needle file—through the puckered end of the pompon and poke a hole through to the other side. Slide the head pin with the end cap on it through the hole. Tip: When you make the hole, put the head pin with the bead cap on it between your lips or on the table within your peripheral vision. When you remove the tool, keep looking at the hole and grab the head pin without removing your eyes from its location. The fuzziness of the fur makes it impossible to ever find the hole if you avert your eyes even for a second!

5 Place a second bead cap on top of pompon, convex side up ❶. Push all the elements firmly against the ballpoint of the head pin. Repeat steps 3 to 5 to make a second component.

APRIL HALE | *Rings*

Fur: opossum, raccoon, squirrel, rabbit

PHOTO BY JOHN LUCAS

GAYLE FRIEDMAN | *Brooch*

Reclaimed mink fur, sterling silver

PHOTO BY JESSICA MARCOTTE

6 Slide a crimp bead onto a head pin and use flat-nose pliers to crimp it. Crimp just the corners of the crimped bead to ensure it really stays on. Repeat on the other component.

7 To make the ear wires, shape the upper ¾ inch (1.9 cm) of each head pin over the barrel of the ballpoint pen. Use pliers to create a small bend at the end of the wire. Attach one to each component.

Variation

All kinds of variations are possible. Experiment with different colors of dyed mink, or look for commercially fabricated fur pompons in a multitude of shades. Make swaying pompons by shortening the head pins and attaching them to lengths of slender chain hung from store-bought ear wires, as shown at top right. Or if you want something sparkly dangling below the pompon (below right), fabricate the earrings with eye pins instead of head pins, to allow you to suspend a looped bead in that spot.

COLLECT

Leather

2 x 4 inches (5.1 x 10.2 cm) of
unvarnished* dyed
garment-tanned leather
flex unimportant 0.8–1.2 mm/2–3 oz.

2 x 4 inches (5.1 x 10.2 cm) of black
oiled vegetable-tanned leather
firm 1.2–1.6 mm/3–4 oz.

Ink pad containing permanent,
non-water-soluble ink

Leather cement

Leather finishing spray

2 jump rings, ¼ inch (6 mm) diameter

2 ear wires

Round drive hole punches in 2 sizes:
• 1¹⁄₂ inches (3.8 cm)
• ³⁄₄ inch (1.9 cm)

3-pound (1.4 kg) mallet

Rubber stamp

Brush

Poly cutting board

2 pairs of small jewelry pliers

*So it will accept the stamped ink.

MAKE

1 Punch two 1½-inch (3.8 cm) circles out of the dyed leather. Punch two circles of the same size from the black oiled leather.

2 Ink up the rubber stamp and press the design down on the grain side of the dyed leather circles.

3 Working in a well-ventilated area, brush the wrong side of all four circles with contact cement. Allow it to predry following the manufacturer's instructions, then press the wrong side of one dyed-leather circle to the wrong side of one black circle, lining up the edges carefully. Repeat with the two remaining circles. Spray the stamped areas of leather with leather finishing spray to protect the prints, and allow it to dry for 20 minutes.

4 Place a glued pair of circles, stamped side up, on the poly cutting board. Position the ¾-inch (1.9 cm) punch ⅛ inch (3 mm) from the edge—anywhere along it is fine—and punch a hole to turn the circle into a hoop. Do the same with the other glued pair.

5 Open a jump ring using two pairs of jeweler's pliers (page 34) and slide a leather hoop onto it, along with an ear wire. Close the jump ring. Repeat to make a second earring.

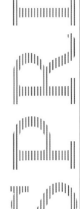

Punch twice, stamp once, and assemble. It takes less time to make these earrings than to pull together the materials and tools.

Design by **Holly Strate**

COLLECT

Leather

6 x 6 inches (15.2 x 15.2 cm) of white garment-tanned leather firm 1.2–1.6 mm/3–4 oz.

6 x 6 inches (15.2 x 15.2 cm) of silver fabric

Fabric or leather glue

Scrap piece of wire

Silver spray paint

Silver paint pen

4 silver jump rings, 6 mm

2 silver ear wires

Small paintbrush

Scissors

Pen

Swivel-head craft knife

Rotating hole punch

2 pairs of needle-nose pliers

MAKE

1 Place the leather wrong side up on your work surface and spread glue completely across it. Immediately place the fabric wrong side down on the leather, matching the edges. Rub to remove any air bubbles, and allow to dry according to the manufacturer's instructions.

2 Copy the template on page 128 and cut it out. Cut away the interior shape. Trace the pattern twice onto the leather, omitting the decorative slits.

3 Cut the exteriors out carefully. Use the swivel-head craft knife to cut out the interior areas.

4 At the center top of each piece of leather, punch out a hole ¹⁄₁₆ inch (1.6 mm)—or as close as possible to that size—referring to the template for placement.

5 Transfer the decorative slit lines from the template onto both leather pieces. Snip them, making sure not to cut all the way through to the interior hole.

6 Hang each leather element on a scrap of wire. Spray paint the front with several coats of the silver spray paint, being careful not to spray the fabric back and allowing the paint to dry completely between coats.

7 After the final coat of spray paint has dried, paint the edges of the leather with the silver paint pen, remembering to get in between the decorative slits, too.

8 Open a jump ring (page 34) with needle-nose pliers and run it through the punched hole in one of the leather pieces. Close it. Attach another jump ring to it, catching one of the ear wires in it before closing it. Repeat step to finish the other earring.

Can't find the right color of leather? No need to complain. Spray it, don't say it!

Design by Joan K. Morris

HOT HUED SCARF 2

Leather

3 x 12 inches (7.6 x 30.5 cm) of pink
garment-tanned goatskin
(or other leather)
very soft 0.8–1.2 mm/2–3 oz.

Pink thread

Open–hoop earrings, 2 1/2 inches
(6.4 cm) in diameter with wire
1/4 inch (6 mm) wide

Pen

Ruler

Shears

Sewing machine with leather needle

Freezer paper

5-minute epoxy

Toothpicks

4 clothespins

MAKE

1 On the wrong side of the leather, use a pen and
ruler to draw two rectangles 1½ x 12 inches
(3.8 x 30.5 cm) and cut them out with shears.

2 Fold the cut pieces in half lengthwise, grain
side out. Machine stitch down the length, ¼ inch
(6 mm) from the fold, making a sort of casing.
(To help the leather move smoothly under the
presser foot, place a piece of freezer paper
between the foot and the leather, waxy side up,
and stitch through all the layers. After stitching,
the freezer paper tears off easily.)

3 Insert the end of an earring—the one without
the post—into one end of a casing, then slide
all of the leather onto the earring, gathering it
as you go and keeping the raw edges facing the
inside of the earring. Arrange the leather so the
gathers are even and the end of the earring wire
lines up with the end of the casing, with the post
sticking out beyond the other end of the casing.
Repeat to cover the other earring in leather.

4 Following the manufacturer's instructions,
mix up a small amount of epoxy. Use a toothpick
to dab epoxy on the inside of the leather casing,
at the end and the post. Pinch the casing ends
closed and place a clothespin over them to hold
them clamped. After the glue has dried, remove
the clothespins.

SCRUNCH

Get noticed! Giant hoops serve as the armature for a scorching hot leather ruffle.

Design by Joan K. Morris

COLLECT

Leather

4 yards (3.7 m) of suede cowhide (or other) lacing, ⅛ inch (3 mm) wide very soft 1.6–2 mm/4–5 oz.

Clear household cement

2 copper beads, 7 mm

2 copper faceted cube beads

2 copper head pins, 2 inches (5.1 cm) long

2 copper ear wires

Pedicure scissors

Ball knot template

2 or 3 toothpicks

Round-nose pliers

Wire cutters

MAKE

1 With pedicure scissors, cut the lacing into four pieces, each 1 yard (91.4 cm) long.

2 Cut one piece of lacing in half. Follow the manufacturer's instructions for the ball knot template ❶. to make a ball with *doubled* lacing. Repeat to make a second ball.

3 Make two more balls, but use just a single strand of lacing for these, to create smaller balls than those made in step 2.

4 Use a toothpick to apply cement to the ends of the lacing at the holes. Allow to dry overnight, then trim off the excess.

5 Slide a 7-mm copper bead, a large suede knot, a faceted cube bead, and a small suede knot onto a head pin. Slip the head pin through the ear wire, loop the end of the head pin with round-nose pliers, and cut off the excess with wire cutters. Repeat for the second earring.

Knot-work is a staple of leatherwork. This contemporary take on the tradition makes it easy by using a commercial knot template.

Design by Nathalie Mornu

COLLECT

Leather

6 x 8 inches (15.2 x 20.3 cm) of orange garment-tanned leather soft 1.2–1.6 mm/3–4 oz.

Leather cement

8 inches (20.3 cm) of orange rat tail cord

2 ear wires

Card stock

Scissors for paper

Shears

1 knitting needle, size 0/2 mm

Black permanent marker

MAKE

1 Copy the templates on page 128, transfer them onto card stock, and cut them out with scissors. Trace them onto the leather in the quantities listed on the templates and cut them out with shears.

2 To make one earring, begin by constructing the bottom element. Fold one of the leather circles in half with the grain facing in, and crease it. Do the same with another circle. Apply cement to one half of each circle, on the wrong side, and press them together, matching the edges. Apply cement to the exposed wrong sides of this construction, and to the wrong sides of two more circles, and press them together with all edges matched. You should end up with something that, from the side, looks like ❶.

Bold earrings call attention to your lovely features. This impressively sculptural pair starts as little more than a dozen circles cut from citrus-hued leather.

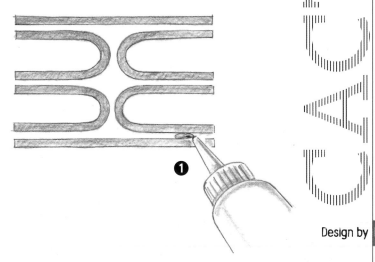

❶

Design by Isabelle Azaïs

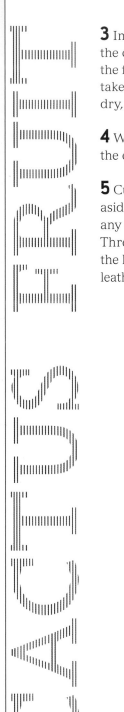

3 Immediately slide the knitting needle through the center, and before the cement dries, fold the flat circles so that, from the top, the element takes on a star shape as shown in ❷. Allow to dry, then remove the knitting needle.

4 With the marker, draw lines prependicular to the edges of the bottom element.

5 Cut the rat tail cord in half and set one piece aside. Using the other piece, tie one end, snip off any excess, and secure it with a dab of cement. Thread the other end through the hole left by the knitting needle and pull the knot close to the leather. Apply a dab of cement to the knot.

6 Make a loop at the other end of the rat tail cord. It needs to be large enough to catch the ear wires later; cut off any excess rat tail. Apply a small quantity of cement to the wrong sides of the ovals cut in step 1 and glue them to each other, catching the rat tail inside with the loop poking out the top ❸. Allow to dry.

7 Hook an ear wire in the loop made from rat tail.

8 Repeat steps 2 through 7 to make the second earring.

Marker lines drawn on the edges of the leather add visual interest.

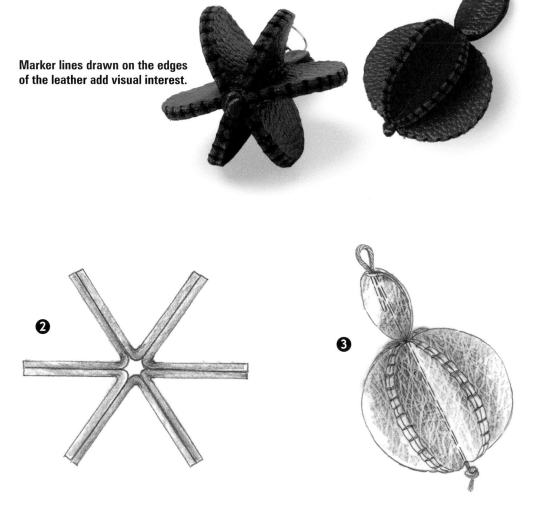

❷

❸

TRILBY HAINSTOCK | *Necklace*

Lizard, metal chain
PHOTO BY ARTIST

ALESSANDRA CALVANI | *Oro Argento, necklace*

Leather
PHOTO BY GILBERTO MALTINTI

MARINA MOLINELLI WELLS | *Pétalos, necklace*

Cow leather, silver
PHOTO BY PABLO MEHANNA

COLLECT

Leather

1 x 1-inch (2.5 x 2.5 cm) scrap of leather for small circle flex unimportant 0.8–1.2 mm/2–3 oz.

1 x 1-inch (2.5 x 2.5 cm) scrap of leather for large circle flex unimportant 1.6–2 mm/4–5 oz.

Leather cement

1 rivet

Pad-topped adjustable ring mount

Black permanent marker, or leather dye

Leather punches in 2 sizes*****:

- $^{7}/_{16}$ inch (1 cm)
- $^{13}/_{16}$ inch (2 cm)

Rotating punch

Mallet

Poly cutting board

*see page 25 for alternative.

MAKE

1 Punch or cut two circles of different colors—one that's $^{7}/_{16}$ inch (1 cm), the other $^{13}/_{16}$ inch (2 cm).

2 With the grain side up on both pieces, center the smaller circle on the larger one, and cement it to that spot. Allow the cement to dry completely.

3 Set the rotating punch to make a hole $^{3}/_{32}$ inch (2 mm) in diameter. Punch a hole in the center of the cemented circles. Mount a rivet (page 26) in the hole using the mallet and poly cutting board.

4 Cement the wrong side of the larger circle to the top of the ring mount.

5 Color the raw edges of the leather with permanent marker or dye.

A carefree design, happy colors, and adjustable ring mount make this finger fashion appeal to young and old alike.

Design by **Géraldine Bailly-Comte**

COLLECT

Fur

1 x 5 inches (2.5 x 12.7 cm) of recycled mink

Embroidery floss in color matching fur

Measuring tape

Chalk

Ruler

Craft knife or shears

Poly cutting board

Needle

MAKE

1 Measure the diameter of the finger and add ¼ inch (6 mm) to that length.

2 On the wrong side of the fur, use chalk and a ruler to draw a rectangle that's ½ inch (1.3 cm) wide by the length determined in step 1.

3 Cut out the rectangle from the wrong side using a craft knife and poly cutting board.

4 Roll the rectangle into a tube and overlap the two ends ¼ inch (6 mm). Using a needle and embroidery floss, hand stitch the ends together with a single knot made through both layers and hidden inside the ring band.

Who says rings have to be made from metal or some hard substance?

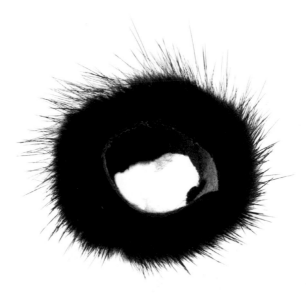

Design by .tomate d'épingles

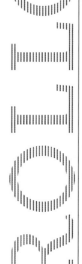

COLLECT

Leather
1 x 5 inches (2.5 x 12.7 cm) of any leather or suede soft 0.8–1.6 mm/2–4 oz.

Embroidery floss

Scissors

Fine-point pen

Poly cutting board

Craft knife or shears

Metal ruler

Paper clip

Needle

MAKE

1 Copy the template on page 124 and cut it out. Put the leather grain side down with the template on it, and trace the outline of the template (but not the dots) with a fine-point pen.

2 Cut the design out of the leather with either a craft knife, using a ruler to keep the lines straight, or with shears.

3 Wrap the leather around the finger and hold it closed with a paper clip. Referring to the placement marks suggested on the template, make two dots on the leather with a fine-point pen to mark where to stitch to fit your size ❶. *Note*: The dots must be very small, smaller than stitching, or they'll show later.

4 Remove the leather carefully from the finger so it keeps its rolled-up shape. With embroidery floss, stitch a knot at each dot, poking the needle through all layers; make a decorative knot to show on the outside of the band and a small double knot on the underside. (The ring can be turned inside out to tie the interior knot.)

Cut a strip of recycled leather, roll it up, and stitch a knot: instant ring. What could be easier?

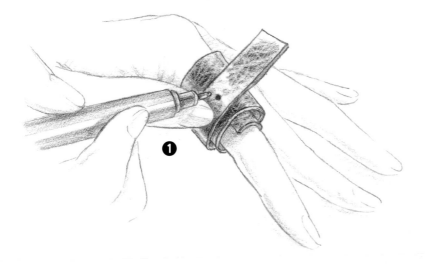

❶

Design by tomate d'épingles

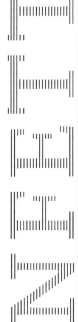

CONFIDENCE

COLLECT

Leather

Recycled leather glove or garment-tanned leather very soft 0.4–0.8 mm/1–2 oz.

40 crimp beads, 2 mm

5 inches (12.7 cm) of bead-stringing wire, 0.024 inch/0.61 mm

Monofilament, 0.010 inch

Ruler

Scissors

Flat-nose pliers

Wire cutters

Hollow punches in 4 sizes:

- ½ inch (1.3 cm)
- ³/₈ inch (1 cm)
- ⁵/₁₆ inch (8 mm)
- ¼ inch (6 mm)

Mallet

Poly cutting board

Tape

Scrap of soft wood

Awl

MAKE

Ring Band

1 String seven crimp beads onto the stringing wire. Form a loop with the wire by passing one end back through all the crimps. Arrange the crimps along the wire to create an element that looks like ❶.

2 To make the finished ring the correct size, slip the loop onto the desired finger and adjust it so it fits comfortably. Removed it carefully so its diameter doesn't change.

3 Let's call the location of the crimps 12:00. Slide the two leftmost beads (labeled 1 and 2) to the 9:00 position. Cut two pieces of monofilament 3 inches (7.6 cm) long. Thread them through the hole in the upper bead—the one numbered 2. With most of the filament pointing vertically above the bead, crimp bead #2 with flat-nose pliers in such a way that the flat plane formed by the crimping is parallel to the ring band formed by the doubled wire, so that it will lie comfortably flat against the finger when worn. (As you work on this step and the next two, refer to ❷, which illustrates the element you should end up with as you finish step 5.)

Splashes of color bob around with every gesture. It will make you want to talk with your hands.

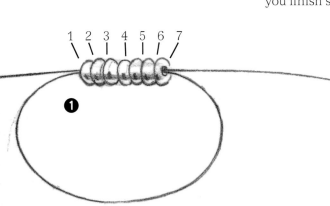

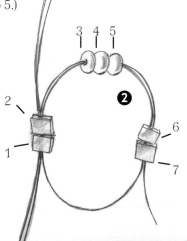

Design by Nathalie Mornu

4 Slide the #1 bead counterclockwise and pull out the loose tail of beading wire; cut off the excess wire, as well as the monofilament, as close as possible to the crimped #2 bead. A tiny bit will remain visible; slide the #1 bead clockwise over it, snug #1 against #2, and crimp it so the flat plane you make aligns with the plane of bead #2.

5 The other side of the band is formed much like in steps 3 and 4, but with the monofilament omitted. Slide beads #6 and #7 to the 3:00 position. Crimp bead #6, creating a flat plane oriented as described in the previous step. Slide bead #7 clockwise and pull out the loose tail of wire. Trim off the excess wire as close as possible to bead #6. Slide bead #7 over whatever tiny bit of wire remains and snugly against #6, then crimp it. You should have something that looks like ❷ (page 89).

Add Monofilament

1 Cut two pieces of monofilament 3 inches (7.6 cm) long. If it has slipped from the 12:00 position, center bead #3 back on that spot, but slide #4 and #5 out of the way. Thread both pieces of monofilament through the hole in #3, center them, and crimp, aiming to make the crimped plane parallel with the curvature of the ring band.

2 Cut three pieces of monofilament 3 inches (7.6 cm) long. Thread them through bead #4 with most of the filament pointing upward, then push the bead snugly against bead #3. Crimp it (don't forget—parallel to the ring band!). Clip off any short tails of filament.

3 Cut a piece of monofilament 3 inches (7.6 cm) long and thread it through bead #5, with most of the filament pointing upward. Snug #5 against bead #4 and crimp it parallel to the band. Snip off the short end of the filament. You should now have a ring band bristling with monofilaments.

Leather Confetti

1 Remove the lining from the glove by cutting all around it at the cuff and pulling it out; slit the glove open along the side seams to create a flat area to punch. Punch four circles of each size from the leather using the mallet and poly cutting board. Set aside.

2 Look over all the monofilament on the ring band to find the one that pokes up the most vertically from the trio of 3-4-5 beads. Attach a tiny bit of tape to its tip.

3 Attach a leather circle to each strand of monofilament—except the one with tape on the end—varying the distance of each circle from the band. To do this, you'll essentially sandwich a circle of leather between two crimps.

Start by placing a leather circle on the scrap of wood and poke the awl through its center to make a hole. Set aside for the moment. Slide a crimp onto any piece of monofilament, then the circle, and finally another crimp bead. Determine the desired placement of the circle and keep it there permanently by crimping both beads directly on either side of it. Trim off any extra filament. You can attach more than one circle of leather to some of the monofilaments. Nor do you have to attach all 16 of the circles you've punched.

4 Remove the tape from the end of the lone, unadorned filament by snipping it off. Attach a leather circle to this piece of filament, sliding the circle directly against the band to camouflage the crimps beneath it. Attach another circle ¼ inch (6 mm) away from it. Trim off any extra filament.

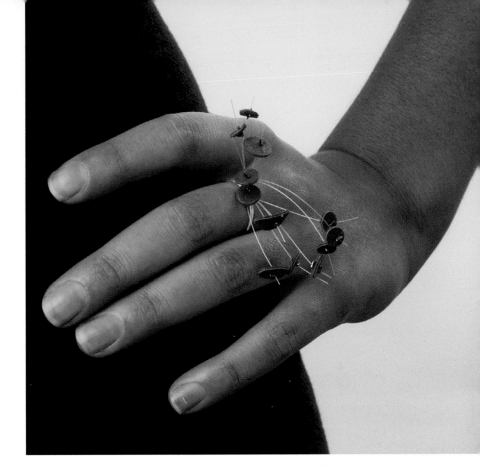

COLLECT

Leather
4 x 8 inches (10.2 x 20.3 cm) of magenta garment-tanned cow suede soft 0.8–1.2 mm/2–3 oz.

Copper leaf, one booklet

Gloss acrylic sealer or medium

Gilding size

Commercial copper patina solution, optional

1 prong snap, copper size 16

Small paintbrush

Soft wide brush

Spoon or burnisher

Fine-point permanent marker, in a shade similar to the suede

Foam brush

Craft knife with fresh blades, or leather knife

Cutting mat

Hole punch or rotary punch

Snap-setting kit

Mallet

Poly cutting board

MAKE

1 You'll begin by affixing the copper leaf to the suede, so make sure to work in a well-ventilated space, and practice on a scrap of suede first. Brush a thin, even coat of acrylic sealer or medium onto the leather. (If it's not thin, it will bleed to the other side.) Brush on a second thin coat to fill any spots you missed the first time, or skip the second coat for a more distressed look.

2 Apply a third coat, this one a thin layer of gilding size. Let it set up, following the manufacturer's instructions.

3 When the size becomes tacky to the touch, it's time to smooth on the copper leaf, which takes a little practice because it's very delicate stuff. Use the booklet of leaf—not your fingers—to guide the material, sliding a little out at a time and working left to right. Once the leaf is on the suede, use a soft brush to smooth the leaf from the center outward ❶. If a few spots are missed, it's easy to patch with smaller pieces of leaf.

Borrow a technique from bookbinders, who apply gold leaf to the covers and spines of fancy leather-bound tomes. Using copper leaf keeps it affordable.

❶

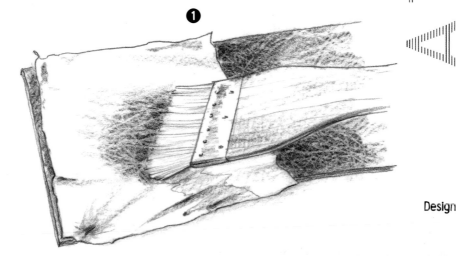

Design by **Trilby Hainstock**

4 Burnish the leaf down with a spoon. The goal is to rub with enough pressure to push the leaf firmly against the suede without tearing it.

5 Finally, seal the leaf with two coats of gloss acrylic sealer applied with a foam brush and let it dry overnight. **Optional**: To create a distressed look, pull the suede gently back and forth over the corner of a table, with the leafed side facing up, to cause the leaf to split slightly, then spritz it with a copper patina solution, following the manufacturer's instructions.

6 Copy the template on page 123 and cut it out. (Check to make sure it fits your wrist, and if not, adjust the enlargement ratio.) With the marker, trace the template onto the leafed side of the suede. Cut it out using a craft knife and a cutting mat, keeping your movements smooth and fluid, and cutting away from the hand holding the work steady. Make sure you've cut away all the trace lines.

7 Referring to the placement indicated on the template, use the hole punch, snap-setting kit, mallet, and poly cutting board to set the snap, making sure the parts face in the correct direction (page 28).

Leaving the back side without leaf means you get two different looks in one bracelet.

LINK

A chain of interconnected elements plays with the leather's texture, mingling the shiny grain side with the velvety sueded face.

Design by Marina Massone

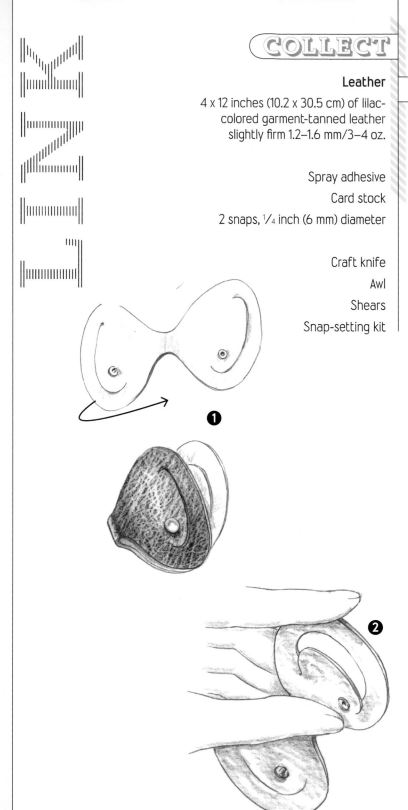

Leather

4 x 12 inches (10.2 x 30.5 cm) of lilac-colored garment-tanned leather slightly firm 1.2–1.6 mm/3–4 oz.

Spray adhesive

Card stock

2 snaps, ¼ inch (6 mm) diameter

Craft knife

Awl

Shears

Snap-setting kit

MAKE

1 Copy the templates on page 124 and glue them to card stock. Cut them out with a craft knife, including the holes and slits.

2 Use an awl to trace the templates onto the leather, grain side up. You'll need four links and one end piece to make a bracelet. With shears and a craft knife, cut out each element, including the holes in the links. Cut slits along the lines marked on the templates.

3 Referring to the placement marks on the template, mount a snap (page 27) on one end piece with the cap element installed on side A so that when the piece is folded and snapped, the grain faces out **❶**.

4 Hold the end piece with its B-side slit open and the wrong side of the leather facing you **❷**. In your other hand, hold a link with the grain facing the end piece and slide its B side through the slit on the end piece **❸**.

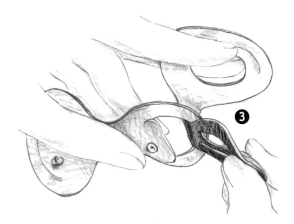

5 Fold the link in half and slide its entire B side into the hole on the A side ❹. Interlace the tongues ❺.

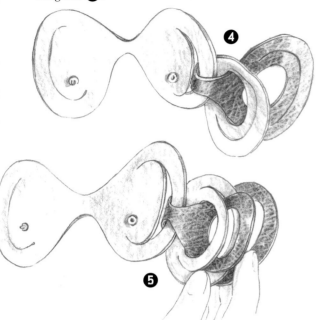

6 Hold the assembled work so the wrong side of the leather in the end piece faces you. Hold a new link with the grain facing the assembled work. Slide the B side of the link through the outermost loop of the assembled work ❻.

7 Repeat steps 5 and 6—inserting the B side of the link into its own A side, interlacing the tongues, and adding the next link—until you've assembled all the links. Don't add a second end piece.

8 The bracelet attaches in the same way it's assembled. After snapping it shut, insert the tongue of the last link into the slit in the end piece ❼ (to avoid muddling the issue, the illustration shows only the pertinent area).

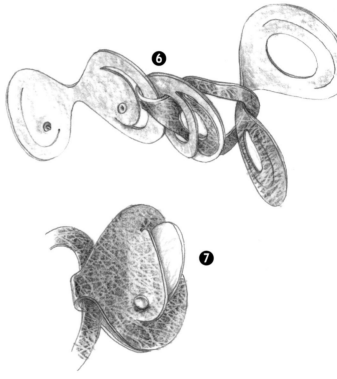

Variation

This design makes a striking necklace, too, as shown at left. Assembling one requires at least 11 links and one end piece. You'll need about 12 x 12 inches (30.5 x 30.5 cm) of leather to make both a necklace and a bracelet.

COLLECT

Leather

12 x 12 inches (30.5 x 30.5 cm)
of garment-tanned cowhide
for the cuff
soft 1.2–1.6 mm/3–4 oz.

1 x 1-inch (2.5 x 2.5 cm) scraps of
leather in different colors
soft 0.8–1.2 mm/2–3 oz.

Double-sided tape

Off-white upholstery thread

2 sets of short-post line 20 snaps

Measuring tape

Ruler

Pen

Shears

Scratch awl

Round punch, ³/₄ inch (1.9 cm)

Sewing machine with a size 16
leather needle

Rotating punch

Poly cutting board

Mallet

Snap anvil

Line 20 snap-setter

MAKE

1 Enlarge the template on page 123. To determine whether it will fit, wrap a tape measure somewhat tightly around the wrist, just above the wrist bone. Ready for a little math? (It won't hurt a bit—promise!)

Add 2 inches (5.1 cm) to your wrist length. If your measurement is larger than 8 inches (20.3 cm)—the length of the template in the book—you'll need to adjust the paper pattern, making it longer by adding half the difference to each side of the rectangle at the dotted line.

For example, if your wrist length is 8½ inches (21.6 cm), adding 2 inches (5.1 cm) to that makes 10½ inches (26.7 cm). The difference between 8 inches (20.3 cm) and 10½ inches (26.7 cm) is 2½ inches (6.4 cm). Half of the difference is 1¼ inches (3.2 cm). At each dotted line, lengthen the template by 1¼ inches (3.2 cm).

2 Tug on the big piece of cowhide to determine which way it stretches. You don't want the finished cuff to stretch, so orient the template on the leather so that the length of the rectangle is perpendicular to the stretchiest direction of the leather. Trace the outline of the template with pen, and cut it out of the leather with shears.

This design is a fun way to combine a range of colors in a playful cuff that works well with any number of outfits.

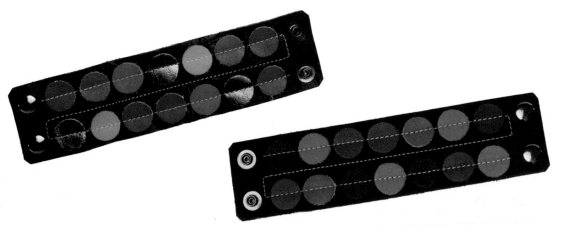

Design by Holly Strate

3 Using the scratch awl, transfer the cross marking the center of each large circle from the template onto the strip of leather; do the same with the broken line indicating where to stitch later. (The markings will disappear when you stitch over them.)

4 Using the pieces of scrap leather, punch out 14 circles. Stick tiny pieces of double-sided tape to the wrong side of each leather dot, then tack them to the grain side of the strip, using the template and the crosses transferred in step 3 as reference.

5 Mount a size-16 leather needle on your sewing machine, thread it with upholstery thread, and set the stitch length to long. Stitch down the circles by following the stitch line transferred from the template. (Each time you reach a corner, stop with your needle in the work, lift the presser foot, swivel, drop the presser foot, and keep sewing.) After stitching, at each end, pull the top thread through to the back and tie a knot.

6 Cut the corners of the strip at a 45° angle. Set the rotating punch to make ⅛-inch (3 mm) holes; referring to the template for placement, punch holes for each snap element. Set the snaps (page 27).

ANDREA JANOSIK | *Pinecone, necklace*

Pigskin, sterling silver

PHOTO BY MAIKE PAUL

PETER MAIN | *Neckpiece*

Cowhide leather, goatskin strap, spirit dyes, concealed magnets

PHOTO BY ARTIST

Grooves cut out of dyed vegetable-tanned leather leave graceful trails. Great on her, perfect for him.

CHANNELS

Design by Holly Strate

CHANGE LANES

Leather
3 x 12 inches (7.6 x 30.5 cm) of vegetable-tanned cowhide firm 3.2–3.6 mm/8–9 oz.

Leather dye

Leather edge dye, color to match leather dye

Leather finishing spray

2 sets of line-20 snaps with long posts

Tape measure

Straightedge

Craft knife

Rubber gloves

Newspaper, or other large, plain paper

Wool dauber

French curve

Stitch groover

1/4-inch (6 mm) flat paintbrush

Edge beveler

Rotary punch

Snap-setting kit

Mallet

Poly cutting board

1 To determine the cuff size, wrap a tape measure somewhat tightly around the wrist, just above the wrist bone. Add 2 inches (5.1 cm) to that measurement.

2 Using the straightedge and craft knife, cut a strip out of the cowhide that's the length figured in the previous step, and 1¾ inches (4.4 cm) wide.

3 Pull on your rubber gloves. Working in a well-ventilated area, and with your work surface protected by a layer of paper, dye the grain side of the strip. To do so, use the wool dauber to apply an even coat without oversaturating the leather, and follow the manufacturer's instructions. Allow to dry for one hour.

4 Place the French curve on the dyed side of the leather, anyplace you like. Using the stitch groover, follow the curved edge, cutting away a line in the dyed surface to reveal the leather's original color. For best results, cut in one smooth stroke without stopping. Repeat, cutting any pattern of lines you like into the leather ❶.

5 Cut all the corners off the cuff at a 45° angle. Using a paintbrush, cover all the edges of the cuff with edge paint and let it dry for 20 minutes.

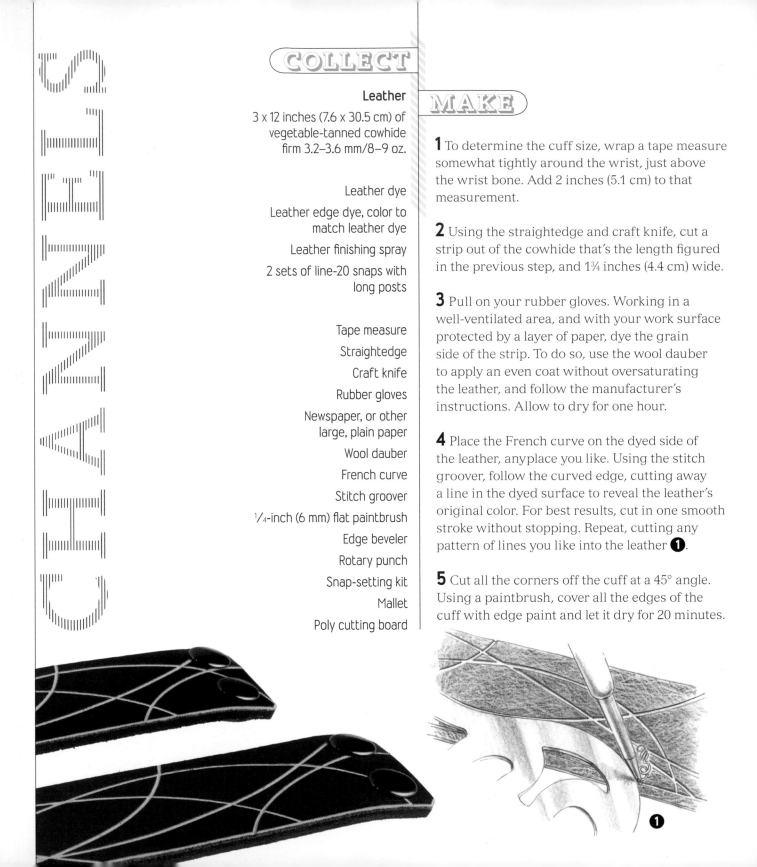

❶

6 On the dyed side of the strip, run the edge beveler at an angle along all the edges. Spray the strip with leather finisher to protect it, and allow it to dry for 20 minutes.

7 Set the rotary punch to make ⅛-inch (3 mm) holes, and mount the snaps using the snap-setting kit, mallet, and poly cutting board (page 27).

COLIN F. GENTLE | *The Links, cuff*
Laser-cut vegetable-tanned leather, brass snaps
PHOTO BY ARTIST

GENEVIEVE GAIL SWINFORD | *Cuffs*
Laser-cut cowhide, elastic
PHOTO BY STEVE MANN

COLLECT

Leather

4 x 18 inches (10.2 x 45.7 cm) of dark purple garment-tanned leather soft 0.4–0.8 mm/1–2 oz.

Rubber cement/spray adhesive

4 x 18 inches (10.2 x 45.7 cm) of paper board or card stock

1 snap

Craft knife

Cutting mat

Ballpoint pen

Shears

Hole punch

Snap-setting kit

Mallet

Poly cutting board

MAKE

1 Enlarge the templates on page 126. Adhere them with rubber cement to the paper board or card stock and cut them out with a craft knife on a cutting mat.

2 Trace the templates with a ballpoint pen onto the wrong side of the leather and cut them out with shears.

3 Fold the tabs on the piece labeled A to the wrong side and glue them down ❶.

4 Fold an oval at either end of A in half lengthwise ❷ and, with both A and B facing grain side up, push it through one of the slots at either end of B ❸.

5 Move to the next oval over on A, fold it in half as described above, and insert it through the next hole over in B. Repeat until the entire bracelet has been assembled.

6 Fold and glue each end tab of A with the matching end tab of piece B between it.

7 Use the hole punch, snap-setting kit, mallet, and poly cutting board to set the snap, trying on the bracelet first to determine the proper placement (page 27).

The honeycomb texture of this bracelet is achieved by a clever design of oval-shaped tabs slipped through slots.

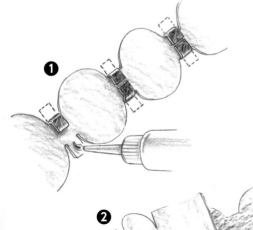

❶

❷

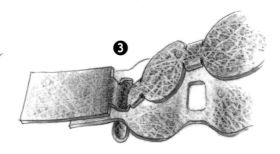

❸

Design by Sarah O'Brien

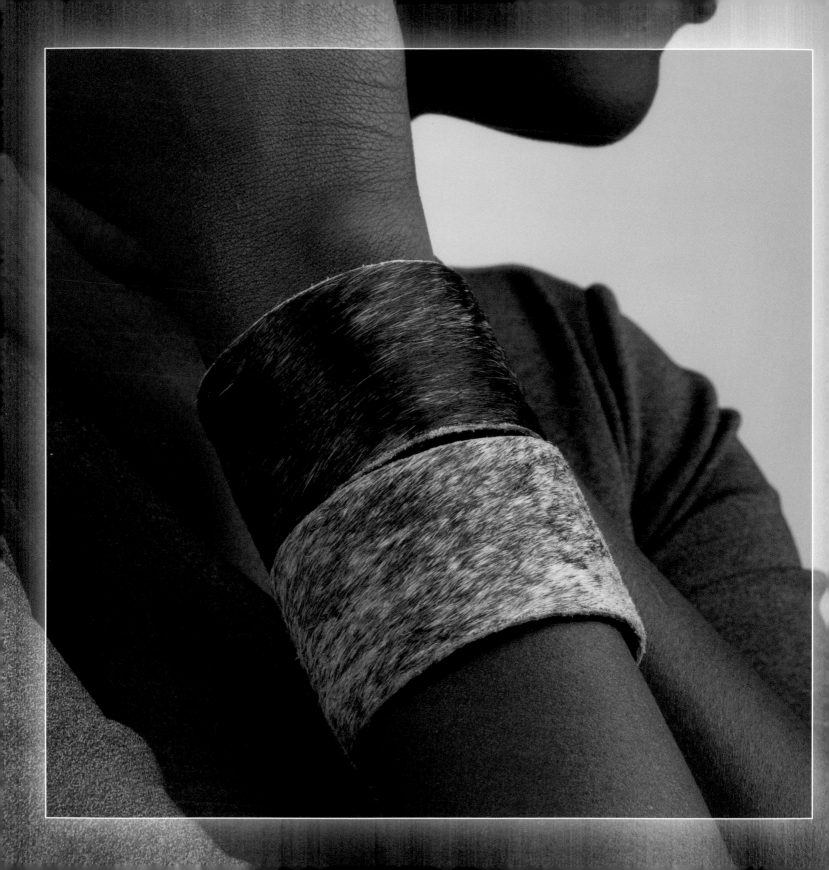

COLLECT

Leather

3 x 10 inches (7.6 x 25.4 cm) of vegetable-tanned cowhide

4 x 11 inches (10.2 x 27.9 cm) of hair-on cowhide firm 1.6–2 mm/4–5 oz.

Leather cement (or any other adhesive available for bonding fabrics)

2 sets of line-20 snaps

Metal ruler

Marker

Cutting mat

Craft knife/cutting blade

Small clamps

Rotary punch

Snap-setting kit

Plastic mallet

Poly cutting board

Tip

Before cutting the leather, make a paper pattern and wrap it around the wrist to double-check that your dimensions are accurate and the finished cuff will fit properly.

MAKE

1 Measure the wrist to determine the desired length and width of your cuff. Add between 1 and 1½ inches (2.5 and 3.8 cm) to the length to allow for the overlap of the snaps.

2 Lay the vegetable-tanned cowhide on your work surface, grain side down, and draw a rectangle with the dimensions determined in step 1. Double-check that both ends are identical in width.

3 Place the leather on a cutting mat. Using a craft knife with a new blade in it and a metal ruler to guide it, cut along the marked lines, applying firm, slow, and steady pressure.

4 Place the hair-on hide on your work surface, fur side down. Lay the leather lining over it (it doesn't matter which side faces up). Draw a wide box around the lining leather, to leave room for handling and cutting errors later, and cut it out.

5 Apply the adhesive to the wrong side of the hide. Spread it in a thin, even layer that reaches just beyond the box you drew.

6 Lay the leather lining carefully within the lines of the box. Smooth it with your hand to make sure that all areas are flat and meet with the hide. Clamp, and allow to dry.

7 Carefully and slowly cut the hide along the edge of the lining, making sure you cut at a perfectly right angle to the flat plane of the leather.

8 Punch a hole on each end of the cuff, 1¼ to 1½ inches (3.2 to 3.8 cm) from the edge, and use the snap-setting kit, mallet, and poly cutting board to set the snaps, making sure the parts face the correct way (page 27).

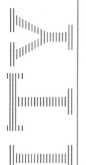

Tough, urban, chic. This cuff lets everyone know you mean business.

Design by UNEARTHED

COLLECT

Leather

7 x 7 inches (17.8 x 17.8 cm) of metallic (or other top-finished) garment-tanned lambskin or pig leather very soft 0.4–0.8 mm/1–2 oz.

Heavy card stock

1 double- or single-prong alligator hairclip, 1 3/4 inches (4.4 cm) long

Craft scissors

Shears

High-temperature glue gun and glue sticks

Medium-grade sandpaper (between 80 and 100 grit)

MAKE

1 Copy the templates on page 125. Transfer the petal patterns onto the card stock and cut them out with scissors.

2 Trace eight large petals, six small petals, one center petal, and one backing onto the leather. Cut them out with shears.

3 On the wrong side of the center petal, apply a line of hot glue to the lower back half, fold the petal lengthwise, and press the sides together. Fold the petal into a cone shape, using a dab of glue to hold it **❶**. Set aside. *Note*: Because the leather has a metallic coating, the glue may not adhere properly; to remedy this, you can roughen any areas where the petals need to stick together with sandpaper.

4 Apply a line of glue along the bottom edge of the grain side of a small petal and wrap it around the cone made in the previous step **❷**. Glue another small petal directly opposite the last one, creating a small bud.

Give the traditional leather flower a contemporary spin by fashioning it in metal hues. Wear it as a hair ornament, as a brooch, or pinned to a hat.

❶

❷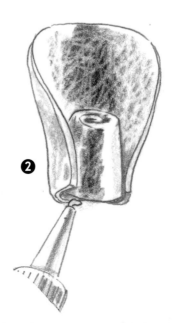

Design by Relle

5 Build the next layer by gluing the rest of the small petals, with the grain facing inside, to the bud ❸, overlapping each in turn and working your way around the central bud as you add each one. Allow the glue to dry completely. Fold the upper edges of the outer petals back, so they look more realistic.

6 If necessary, trim the base of the bud slightly to flatten it. Spread glue over the base and stick the grain side of the point of a large petal to its center. Glue three more large petals in the same manner to the cardinal points of the base ❹.

7 Wet the edges of each petal with water, using your fingers. While they're damp, shape and form each petal by rolling the edges between your fingers ❺. Allow to dry. If desired, secure the petals in place by putting a dab of glue on the inner sides of the large petals and sticking each to the bud. This gives a more realistic appearance and prevents the flower from flattening out later.

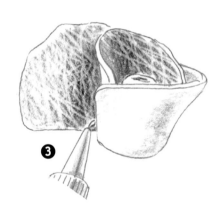

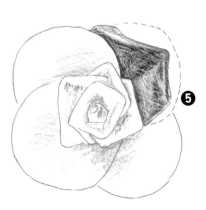

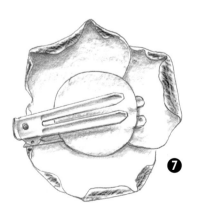

8 Glue the remaining four large petals around the base of the rose as shown in **6**. After the glue has completely hardened, form and shape these petals as described in step 6, and secure them to the previous layer. Allow the glue to dry.

9 Apply glue to the grain side of the backing. Hold the hairclip open and stick the backing perpendicular to the underside of the upper clip, then press the backing to the base of the rose **7**.

COLLECT

Leather

2 x 3 inches (5.1 x 7.6 cm) of unvarnished* light-colored garment-tanned leather slightly firm 0.8–1.2 mm/2–3 oz.

Paper or card stock

Pencil

Black permanent ink (non-water soluble) and ink pad

Leather finishing spray

3 inches (7.6 cm) of black wire, 26 gauge

1 metal hair clip with a hole at each end, 2 inches (5.1 cm) long

Scissors

Rubber stamp with a pattern of leaf veins

Corkboard

Awl

Wire cutters

Small jewelry pliers

*So it will accept the stamped ink.

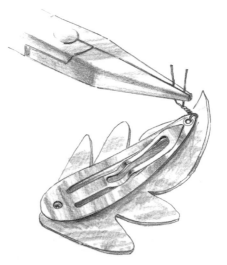

MAKE

1 Copy the template on page 128, transfer it (including the four little dots) onto the paper or card stock, and cut it out.

2 With pencil, trace the outline of the paper pattern onto the leather, and cut out the leaf shape.

3 Ink up the rubber stamp and press it down onto the leather. Being sure to work in a well-ventilated area, spray the shape with a leather finisher to protect the print, and allow to dry for 20 minutes.

4 Place the paper template on the back of the leather leaf shape, lining up the edges carefully, and on the wrong side of the leather, mark the placement of the four holes, shown as dots on the template. Place the leaf shape on the corkboard and use the awl to poke the holes where marked.

5 Cut the wire in half. On the grain side of the leaf, at one end, feed one piece of wire through the holes. With the leaf grain side down and the hair clip right side down, run one end of the wire through the hole in the hair clip. Twist the two ends of wire tightly with jewelry pliers , trim away the excess, and tuck the ends under the clip. Repeat on the other side to attach the other half of the leaf to the hair clip.

Use a rubber stamp with a leaf motif to embellish barrettes fit for a woodland fairy.

Design by Holly Strate

COLLECT

Leather

4 x 21 inches (10.2 x 53.3 cm) of black
garment-tanned leather
very soft 0.8–1.2 mm/2–3 oz.

8 glass pearls, 10 mm

5 glass pearls, 8 mm

7 glass pearls, 5 mm

Thread in color matching the leather

Fabric glue

20 inches (50.8 cm) of black elastic,
$1/_8$ inch (3 mm) thick

Sewing machine with leather needle

Scissors

Ruler

Freezer paper

Sturdy hand-sewing needle (the eye
must pass through the beads)

Shears

Toothpick

MAKE

1 Mount a leather needle in your sewing machine. Enlarge the template on page 125. Cut it out and set it aside.

2 To make the ridges, start working at one end of the piece of leather; measure in 2 inches (5.1 cm) from the short edge and make a fold with the wrong sides together. Machine stitch as close as you can to the fold; to help the leather move smoothly under the presser foot, place a piece of freezer paper on top of the leather, waxy side up. The freezer paper tears away easily after stitching.

3 Continue folding and stitching your way across the entire piece of leather, alternating the distances between the ridges as well as the angles in relation to the long edge of the leather. They can be anywhere from ½ to 2 inches (1.3 to 5.1 cm) apart and don't need to run parallel. The strip should not get any shorter than 15 inches (38.1 cm).

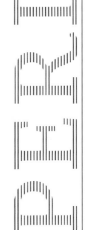

From ratty old leather mini to new leather headband: would you call that skirting the issue, or being headstrong?

Design by Joan K. Morris

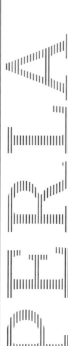

4 Lay the ridged piece flat and decide where to place the pearls. As you do, lay the template over them to make sure the pearls will be attached within its outline. Hand sew the beads in place with a sturdy needle and matching thread. (Stitch through holes that are already there from the line of machine stitching used to make the ridges, and this step will be so much easier.) Stitching on the pearls may distort the shape of the leather, so keep checking the bead placement against the template outline. (No point sewing on beads that will get cut away in the next step, right?)

5 Using the template as a guide, cut out the leather with shears.

6 To ensure the seams don't unravel, dab fabric glue—if you put it on the end of a toothpick, you can get really accurate—onto the end of each row of stitching, as well as on the stitching holding on the pearls. Set aside and allow to dry completely.

7 Fold over one end of the leather, as marked on the template, and machine stitch it to make a casing. Do the same on the other end of the leather. Thread the elastic through the casings ❶. Try on the headband to determine the required length of the elastic, and cut away any excess. Hand sew the ends of the elastic together, then slide the seam inside the nearest casing. Keep it there by machine sewing it down. To keep the visible elastic looking neat, hand sew it side by side in three spots, as shown in.

❶

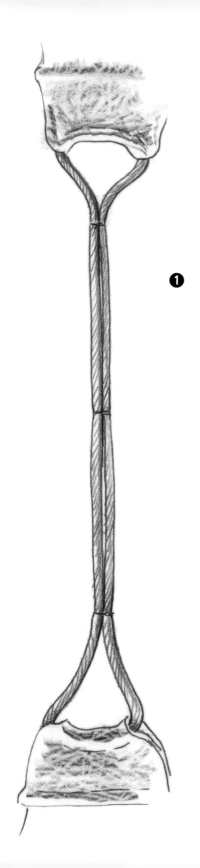

Gallery

BIRGIT LAKEN | *Necklace*

Goatskin on copper/zinc alloy,
gold, blood coral
PHOTO BY GERHARD JAEGER

ISABELLE AZAÏS | *Brooch*

Leather, silver
PHOTO BY ARTIST

NANCY WORDEN | *Necklace*

Mink fur, silver, brass, pearls,
glass, steel, mother-of-pearl
PHOTO BY REX RYSTEDT

GINTA SICEVA | *Brown Daisy, earrings*
Leather, glass beads
PHOTO BY VALTS KLEINS

COLIN F. GENTLE
(COLIN-FRANCIS DESIGN, CUFFMODERN) | *Encircled, choker*
Laser-cut vegetable-tan
leather, brass snaps
PHOTO BY ARTIST

MAYUMI MATSUYAMA | *Bracelet*
Cowhide, silver
PHOTOS BY HIDEYUKI NOMA

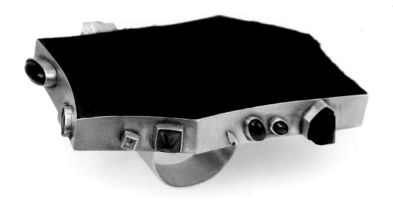

KADRI MÄLK | *Hunting Field, ring*

Moleskin, silver, rubber, stones,
shark tooth

PHOTO BY TŰT RAMMUL

MICHAELA BINDER | *Ring*

Mink fur, freshwater pearl,
gold-plated silver

PHOTO BY ARTIST

AARON SAULT | *Rings*

Red squirrel fur, rabbit fur,
sterling silver

PHOTO BY ARTIST

BARBARA COHEN | *Brooch*

Fox fur, silk cocoons, rivets,
paint, magnets

PHOTO BY ARTIST

MAARJA NIINEMÄGI | *Brooches*

Formed leather, titanium, copper, gold

PHOTOS BY ARTIST

UNEARTHED
(KAREN AND GINA KOENIG) | *Cuffs*

Dyed calfskin, metal

PHOTO BY KAREN KOENIG

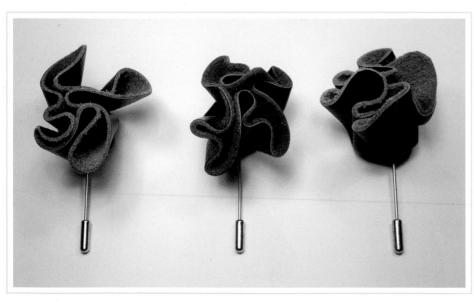

CHARLOTTE FILSHIE | *Brooches*

Cowhide, silver

PHOTO BY ARTIST

RUTH AVRA | *Rings*

Stingray, leather, sterling silver
PHOTO BY ARTIST

**UNEARTHED
(KAREN AND GINA KOENIG)** | *Bangles*

Dyed snakeskin, plastic/resin
PHOTO BY KAREN KOENIG

TANIA CLARKE HALL | *Earrings*

Cowhide, silver, paint
PHOTO BY PAUL KING

PAT PRUITT | *Cuff*
//////
Stingray, stainless steel
PHOTO BY ARTIST

ANASTASIA KANDARAKI | *Necklace*
//////
Cowhide, silk thread, cotton
PHOTO BY FEDERICO CAVICCHIOLI

ANDREA JANOSIK | *Red Roll, necklace*
//////
Sheepskin, sterling silver,
leather cord
PHOTO BY MAIKE PAUL

Templates

Arabesque, page 92
Actual size

Snap placement

Snap placement

Polka, page 98
Actual size

Snap placement

Snap placement

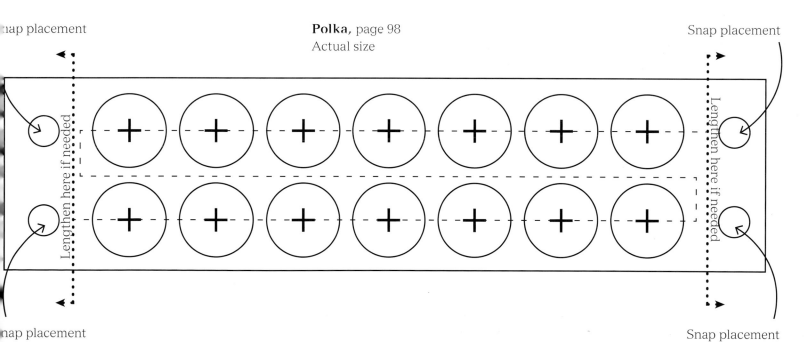

Lengthen here if needed

Lengthen here if needed

Snap placement

Snap placement

Fog, page 56
Enlarge 200%

Grommet placement

Grommet placement

Rollo, page 86
Actual size

Suggested hole location

Suggested hole location

Link, page 95
Actual size

Link

Slit

B side

A side

Slit

End piece

Slit

Snap placement

B side

A side

Snap placement

Slit

leam, page 108
ctual size

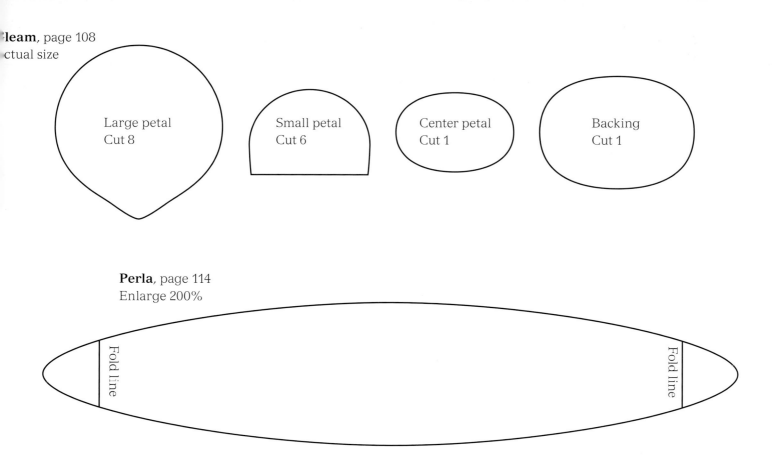

Large petal
Cut 8

Small petal
Cut 6

Center petal
Cut 1

Backing
Cut 1

Perla, page 114
Enlarge 200%

Fold line

Fold line

Luna, page 62
Actual size

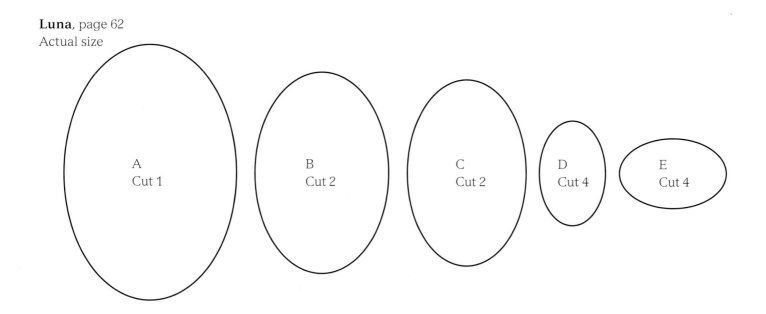

A
Cut 1

B
Cut 2

C
Cut 2

D
Cut 4

E
Cut 4

DiscoBoa, page 48
Actual size

Center

End

Aubergine, page 104
Enlarge 200%

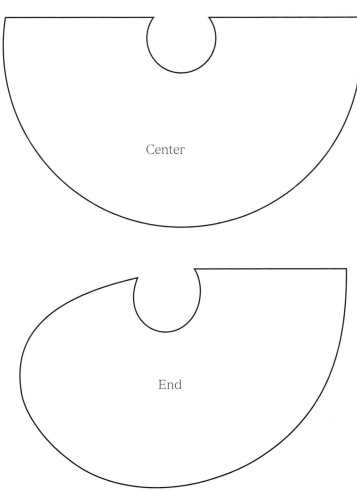

B

A

Once assembled together, these templates create a series of interlocked hills and valleys 6¾ inches (17.1 cm) long; the tabs where the snap is mounted make the bracelet a little longer than that. To change the length of the finished piece, lengthen or shorten the tabs on the template labeled A.

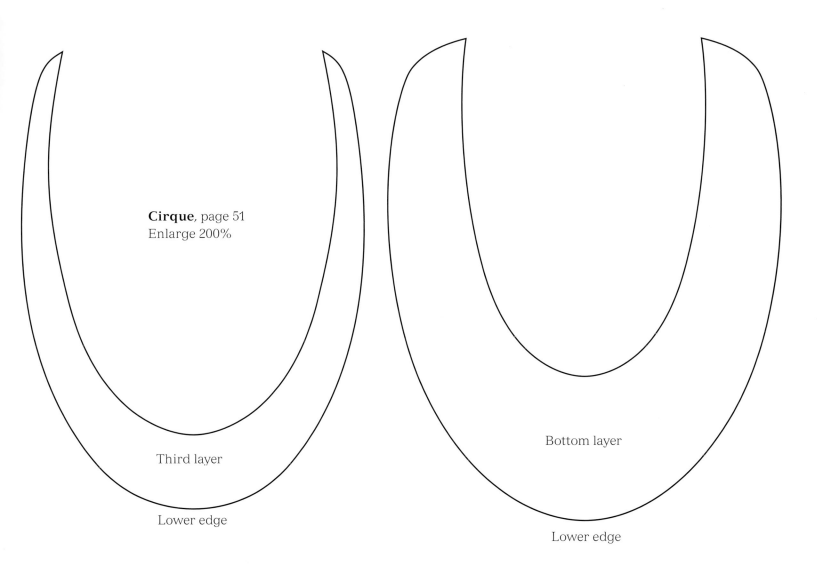

Cirque, page 51
Enlarge 200%

Third layer

Lower edge

Bottom layer

Lower edge

Cactus Fruit, page 78
Actual size

Cut 12

Cut 4

Tassel, page 64
Actual size

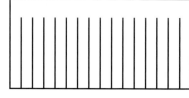

Long tassel
Cut 2

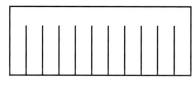

Short tassel
Cut 2

Graffiti, page 72
Actual size

Decorative slits

Leaflet, page 112
Actual size

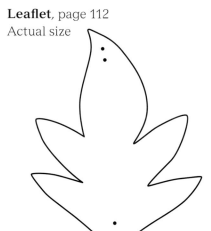

About the Designers

Natacha Amblard (Coco, page 39) creates a wide variety of jewelry, following her inspiration as she comes across interesting raw materials. She lives in France and maintains a website at www.crea-bijoux.fr, where you can view more of the line she fashions from leather cord.

Isabelle Azaïs (Cactus Fruit, page 78; Luna, page 62) was born in Toulouse, France. After studying fine art and doing ten years of painting, sculpting, and installations work, she moved to Brussels, Belgium, in 2000, where she opened a centrally located studio/showroom called La Vitrine (The Window) in 2006. Isabelle now works solely in leather, creating modern jewelry. She shows her work in the fashion world as well as in fine art galleries, and groups her collections within three categories: haute couture, ready-to-wear, and experimental work made of recycled materials. She collaborates regularly with the costume departments of theater groups. Visit her website at www.azais.be.

Géraldine Bailly-Comte (Dot, Dot, Dot, page 82) makes her living crafting leather goods—including billfolds, purses, instrument cases, and home decor items—in France. After working in the fashion industry, she set up her own studio in the Drôme region, in the southern part of the country. All of her wares are handmade and respect the traditions of leatherworking. You can see more of Géraldine's work at www.selleriedeslyres.com, or write her at contact@selleriedeslyres.com.

Paula Darnell (Lassoo, page 42) teaches jewelry making, as well as writing, at the College of Southern Nevada. As a maker of jewelry, Paula is fascinated with the myriad possibilities of innovation in its design, and she finds inspiration in colors, textiles, crafting techniques, and vintage jewelry. She enjoys combining unusual materials and techniques to create new pieces. Paula maintains an active interest in all aspects of fashion, from fashion history to current trends. She collects vintage jewelry and is the author of *Victorian to Vamp: Women's Clothing 1900–1929*. As About.com's Guide to Petite Fashion, Paula writes about fashion for short women; read her column at http://petite.about.com and see more of her work on her website, www.pauladjewelry.com.

Trilby Hainstock (Arabesque, page 92) received her BFA from California College of the Arts in San Francisco, and now lives in Seattle, where she works as a theatrical scenic artist. Her artwork includes paintings and prints, jewelry, really big murals, mini frescos, motion lamps, and live performance paintings with ChromaMatic. She enjoys collaborating with other artists and is excited about DIY culture keeping the art of craft alive and accessible. Trilby can be contacted at TrilbyMade@etsy.com.

Eleanore Macnish (Pom, page 67) has been a beadmaker for 13 years and a silversmith for four. She honed her skills at the Studio at Corning Glass, has studied with Paul Stankard at Urban Glass in New York, and was a studio assistant to Emily Brock. Her work has been exhibited in museums and galleries across the country and is published in numerous books and magazines. Eleanore is a regular contributor to *Jewelry Artist Magazine* (formerly *Lapidary Journal*) and *Bead Unique Magazine*. She's represented by Mariposa Gallery (Albuquerque) and La Mesa Gallery (Canyon Road, Santa Fe). Originally from Topeka, Kansas, Eleanore graduated with a degree in anthropology from the University of Kansas. She currently lives in Albuquerque and works exclusively as a studio artist. Visit her website at www.emacnish.com.

Marina Massone (Link, page 95) was born in Argentina. She teaches industrial design at the University of Buenos Aires; she also runs a workshop called "Design and Production of Contemporary Jewellery." Marina explores the formal and technical possibilities of materials to create modular pieces, curved three-dimensional shapes that are articulated to form flexible metallic structures that move on the body. Marina has exhibited her work in numerous national and international exhibitions, art galleries, design fairs, and museums in New York, Shanghai, Italy, Spain, Argentina, and the United Kingdom. With 12 other Argentine designers, she was selected to partic-ipate in "Destination: Buenos Aires. New Argentine Design," which exhibited at the Museum of Modern Art in New York. Marina's website is www.marinamassone.com.ar; contact her at info@marinamassone.com.ar.

Sara McCormick (Fog, page 56) grew up in Oregon. In high school, she developed a fasci-nation with the natural world and with scientific exploration, and fell in love with the amazingly rich variety of forms and patterns found in nature. Sara then astonished all her friends by enrolling in art school! She received a BFA in fiber arts from the Maryland Institute College of Art in 2005. In the sculptural and functional art she creates, inspiration continues to come from myriad natural forms and patterns, and the rich, sensual nature of materials like leather and stone are at the heart of many of her designs. She strives for an organic feel, as if the pieces had grown or evolved rather than been constructed. Sara lives in Portland, Oregon, where she makes a meager living as Infinite Creature Designs, selling her art at the Portland Saturday Market and online at infinitecreature. etsy.com, as well as doing custom design work and consulting. Visit her website, www.infinitecreature. net, or contact her at infinitecreature@gmail.com.

Joan K. Morris (Big Zip, page 46; Cirque, page 51; Graffiti, page 72; Perla, page 114; Scrunch, page 74) has gone down many creative paths, including costume design for motion pictures, and ceramics. She has contributed projects to numerous Lark books, including *Quilt It with Wool* (2009), *50 Nifty Beaded Cards* (2008), *Button! Button!* (2008), *Pretty Little Potholders* (2008), *Cutting-Edge Decoupage* (2007), *Extreme Office Crafts* (2007), and many, many more.

Delphine Muller (Tassel, page 64) started making jewelry 15 years ago, while in college. The pieces were crafted from electric cables, old jewels, and polymer clay. She has just finished her studies (not in art!), and she continues to create work, but now it's a little bit different, more feminine or perfected. Above all, her pleasure is to come up with novel ideas and find new combinations. For the time being, elaborate jewelry is her only passion. Delphine lives in Alsace, France. Check out her blog, where you can see more of her designs, at lavaqueria.canalblog.com. Her email address is chou_bijoux@hotmail.fr.

Sarah O'Brien (Aubergine, page 104) has been creating objects since she received her first origami book at age four. A passion for design led her to pursue a degree in product design. She currently works in New York City, where she divides her time between 212box Architecture, where she's establishing a product design division that focuses on furniture and lighting, and her own consulting company, obrien-design.com. Her work has won numerous national awards and has been featured in many media outlets, including the *New York Times*, the *Christian Science Monitor*, and MSN.com.